THE QS-9000 BOOK

THE FAST TRACK TO COMPLIANCE

JOHN T. RABBITT & PETER A. BERGH

QUALITY RESOURCES.
A Division of The Kraus Organization Limited
New York, New York

Most Quality Resources books are available at quantity discounts when purchased in bulk. For more information contact:

Special Sales Department
Quality Resources
A Division of the Kraus Organization Limited
902 Broadway   800-247-8519
New York, New York 10010   212-979-8600
www.qualityresources.com   E-mail: info@qualityresources.com

Printed in the United States of America

02 01 00 99 98   10 9 8 7 6 5 4 3 2 1

Quality Resources   This book is distributed by:
A Division of the Kraus Organization Limited   AMACOM Books, a division of
902 Broadway   American Management Association
New York, New York 10010   1601 Broadway
800-247-8519   New York, New York 10019
212-979-8600

                          ∞

The paper used in this publication meets the minimum requirements of American National Standard for Information Sciences—Permanence of Paper for Printed Library Materials, ANSI Z39.48-1984.

ISBN 0-527-76334-9 (Quality Resources)
ISBN 0-8144-7982-0 (AMACOM)

Library of Congress Cataloging-in-Publication Data

Rabbitt, John T.
    The QS-9000 book : the fast track to compliance / John T. Rabbitt, Peter A. Bergh.
        p.   cm.
    Includes index.
    ISBN 0-527-76334-9 (Quality Resources: cloth : alk. paper)
    ISBN 0-8144-7982-0 (AMACOM: cloth : alk. paper)
    1. QS-9000 (Standard) 2. Automobiles—Parts—Design and construction—Quality control—Standards—United States. 3. Automobile industry and trade—Quality control—Standards—United States. I. Bergh, Peter A. II. Title.
TL278.5.R33   1997
629.2'34—dc21   97-27673
                                                       CIP

To the employees of Span Instruments, who took up the challenge of going from ground zero to compliance in 5½ months and made this book possible.

To George Yurch, president, and Don Whitson, owner, of Span Instruments for their wisdom and total commitment to this quality effort. To Peter Claypool, Peter Kayfus, Kevin MacGibbon, Rod Madsen, Bryce Drake, Anne Sisk, Mary Borrego, Shannon Womble, and many others for all their sweat and effort.

And especially to our spouses Charlotte and Deborah and children Beth, Ciara, Emelie, Natalie, and Julia, and our families for making this endeavor possible.

Contents

List of Figures

Introduction
How Did We Get Here?

QS-9000 has been promoted as a life preserver for the automotive industry. Some of its intended users have referred to it as the iron life preserver. At first glance, you may feel like you are about to drown in another round of bureaucracy at the expense of the relationship you have
with your customer.

QS-9000 is more than just a standard handed down by the automotive giants with a mandate to comply or die. It is a quality tool, which
when properly deployed, yields a well-organized operation with trained
and motivated people who have thoroughly thought through their products and processes. The result is greater customer satisfaction and an improved bottom line. Companies who embark on the QS-9000 journey
should understand that it will create organizational stress, but ignoring
this latest improvement tool is most likely a far worse option. This new
challenge is just one of an ongoing series of competitive hurdles that
manufacturers and service providers face moving into the 21st century.

The principles behind QS-9000 aren't new. In Henry Ford's 1926
book, *Today and Tomorrow,* he says, "Our own attitude is that we are
charged with discovering the best way of doing everything, and that we
must regard every process employed in manufacturing as purely exper-
imental. If we reach a stage in production which seems remarkable as
compared with what has gone on before, then that is just a stage of production and nothing more. It is not and cannot be anything more than
that. We know from changes that have already been brought about that
far greater changes are to come, and that therefore we are not performing a single operation as well as it ought to be performed."

Henry Ford understood the concept of continuous improvement
that the automotive industry has had to relearn. They have responded
by setting higher standards for performance (internally and externally)

to prevent the largesse of the '60s and the disasters of the '70s while preserving the hard won gains of the late '80s and '90s. They have heard Deming's message and understand they can only improve when their suppliers grow with them. Consequently, they have taken the firm position that they will do business only with companies that deploy resources and commit to a quality direction consistent with QS-9000. Those who move quickly will enjoy the fruits that come from being a leader. Those who defer will feel the pain of lost business. Companies that do not enjoy a direct or indirect relationship with the automotive industry can also benefit from QS-9000 compliance as it is an excellent device for getting closer to meeting the requirements of the Malcolm Baldrige National Quality Award. Beyond that, QS-9000 is about running your organization guided by good common sense business principles and techniques which have been around for most of this century.

To put QS-9000 in its proper perspective it is useful to examine how manufacturing and the requirements for QS-9000 have evolved. It is ironic that our grandparents were in fact performing much of what is being touted as a new requirement (QS-9000).

ENLIGHTENED MANUFACTURING

Much earlier in this century, Henry Ford saw a different way of conducting business. He expounded on the ideas of continuous improvement and waste reduction. In his book, *Today and Tomorrow,* written in 1926, he discussed how the concepts of process and linked flows were introduced and practiced. Ford drove his organization to continually look at the entire process and to continually work to improve each step. He knew his business and insisted that his employees do the same.

Ford felt that his employees and customers were one and the same, and unless an organization took care of its employees as well as its customers, it would destroy itself. He also believed that satisfying his customers was the greatest service he could provide, that satisfaction came from a continually lower cost of ownership, and that the world belonged to those who provided this service.

In 1908, the first Model T was introduced at a material cost of $850 and by 1924 he had not only dramatically improved the reliability of the vehicle, but had driven the material costs down to $290. Ford finished production of the Model T in 1927 and had sold more than 15 million units.

Ford also pioneered the concepts of Process Integrity, Total Quality Control, Just In Time (JIT), and Kanban feed systems. He never allowed more than one shift's worth of material on the assembly floor. "Our production cycle is about 81 hours from the mine to the finished machine in the freight car." Today, that is about how long it takes to move the average material through incoming inspection. Ford also established the concepts of waste of inventory, energy conservation, employee training, employee safety, and cleanliness on the job site.

When asked to give advice to someone starting out (and the reason for his success), Ford said, "If we do that which is before us to do in the best way that we know, that is, if we faithfully try to serve, we do not have to worry about anything else. The future has a way of taking care of itself."

Meanwhile, in 1924, a 33-year-old engineer named Walter Shewart, who studied the statistical teachings of 19th century Englishman Sir Ronald Fisher, gave birth to the "Process Control Chart," at another bastion of American industry, the infamous Western Electric, Hawthorn Plant. The Hawthorn Plant was America's "High Tech" facility of its day, employing up to 40,000 people of which 5,200 were in the quality department charged with finding and fixing the problems (scary, isn't it?). Shewart demonstrated that by the use of statistical theory, a manufacturing operation could discover and measure the effects of unknown causes on the manufacturing system. He eventually became the father of Quality Control and his Process Control Charts are very much in use today. Walter Shewart also defined the "State of Control" and first defined quality in terms of "Human Values." Mr. Shewart later worked with and taught the quality gurus, Deming and Juran. Shewart laid the founding principles of quality, as we understand it today.

In other American bastions, individuals such as Allan Morganson of Kodak, were discovering that the people who were doing the work knew the most about the job and that they should be treated with respect listened to, and should be involved in the simplification of the manufacturing process they worked in. He is credited with the saying "Work smarter, not harder" and it was his findings that would later become the foundation for work groups and cross-functional improvement teams.

THE BOOM YEARS

After Ford created his eighth wonder of the world, bankers and stock-brokers began the process of speculation and uncontrolled borrowing. Meanwhile, the public adopted the Roaring '20s mindset of "live for to-day." This nonproductive activity eventually caused the collapse of the capital market and drove the country into the depression of the 1930s.

For the next 10 years people lived conservatively. As World War II created a new demand for goods as well as shortages, the U.S. economy began to recover. The government created war-related jobs and rationed consumer goods to keep inflation down while participating in the de-struction of a large segment of the world's industrial capacity. By the end of World War II, the U.S. had enjoyed 4 years of full employment. However, the little opportunity for consumer spending created an enor-mous capital base and a high demand for consumer goods. The U.S. Government then lent money to select war-ravaged countries to buy goods from the only remaining intact industry base, which was the U.S.

This resulted in an unparalleled shortage of goods. New inexperi-enced manufacturers emerged as a result of the shortages and product quality continued to decline. For example, the Kaiser-Frazer Auto Company was founded when a liberty ship builder teamed up with Joseph Frazer, a very successful car salesman from Packard and Gen-eral Motors. Although the car they developed did have some innovative features, they still had not overcome technical issues such as hard steer-ing, gear whine, and wheel shimmy. However, when the car was intro-duced, it sold as if there was no tomorrow. Demand subsided in the early 1950s, marking the demise of Kaiser-Frazer. The motto of the 1950s and 1960s was "Make the Schedule." This worked quite nicely for the U.S. economy as it grew at an extraordinary rate. Then in the mid-1960s, German "bugs" started popping up everywhere, followed by a series of Japanese "beetles."

THE JAPANESE LISTENED

World War II destroyed Japan's industrial base. It actually employed a recovery strategy that typifies most growing nations, and there are clear transition points. In the 1950s, Japan focused on low-cost, labor-intensive, low technology industries like textiles. Meanwhile, U.S. quality gurus Deming and Juran were teaching lessons on process control and management throughout Japan.

During the 1960s, the Japanese had amassed enough capital to engage in a large scale manufacturing based strategy that focused on productivity improvements. During the 1970s they developed flexible manufacturing strategies that incorporated both the "scales" strategy with the "variety" approach. Meanwhile, cheap labor was becoming a thing of the past. Japanese industry was moving beyond Ford's concepts into new frontiers. Concurrently, the U.S. was becoming infatuated with computers and their promise of effortless salvation.

"Listen to me, and in 5 years you will be competing with the West. Keep listening, and soon the West will be demanding protection from you."

—W. Edwards Deming, speaking to 45 key
Japanese industrialists at a seminar in 1950

American industry believed the computer salvation story until the late 1980s. Ironically, during the early 1980s, the computer industry was already in the process of replacing massive computer-driven shop floor control systems with JIT and Kanban, but they weren't telling, lest they shoot the golden goose. In fact, a computer-industry pioneer was told not to make a speech at an industrial conference on JIT for fear of damaging the industry. The U.S. was losing the race and it wasn't until the late 1970s that the lessons learned by the Japanese started beating the daylights out of our industries. The weak players were the first to feel the impact.

THE DECLINING YEARS

In 1979, the Ford Motor Company recalled more cars than it produced. In consumers' eyes, "Ford" became an acronym for "Fix or Repair Daily" and Ford's customers were getting a "Better Idea" from the competition. The effect on the business was devastating, thousands were laid off, and industry observers were wondering if they were witnessing the demise of the Founding Father of the automotive industry. Meanwhile, our consumer electronics industry was rapidly migrating offshore. According to U.S. Labor Department statistics, during the mid-1980s, many new jobs were created, giving the illusion that the economy was on an even keel. But these were low-wage service sector jobs, and the U.S. was losing 20,000 to 30,000 manufacturing jobs a month to foreign manufacturing.

In 1980, Ford executives asked Dr. Deming to come in and breathe some life into their failing entity. Dr. Deming gave them some very sound advice that began with knowing their process and gaining stability within their operation. By the mid-1980s, the Japanese were evolving their "variety and speed" strategy. General Motors (GM) had determined that they would automate out of existence the very thing that Ford had considered his most valuable asset—people. GM made a big bet on strategies such as MAP (manufacturing automation protocol) as the answer to this latest competitive challenge, even though there was clear evidence that the organizations that were beating them in the marketplace were employing a different approach.

> *"You can always count on the Americans to do the right thing!
> . . . but, only after they have tried everything else . . ."*
>
> —Winston Churchill

By 1985, Ford had achieved a remarkable rebound and had just out-earned GM. By 1987, Ford boosted profits by an additional 40%. What caused this remarkable turnaround? Ford gained control of its processes and met a minimum set of customer expectations, which is the essence of QS-9000.

THE SHOT HEARD 'ROUND THE WORLD

In the 1980s, the Europeans banded together to create the world's largest market with new barriers and hopes for a revival of European competitiveness. The Asian basin was afire with development and growth. The International Organization for Standardization (ISO) supported a growing recognition for the need to rethink how businesses compete and how to protect the consumer. The Europeans, understanding the need for a level playing field for competition, adopted the ISO 9000 standard in 1987 as a mandatory requirement for certain products, and the race for ISO 9000 certification was on. By the mid-1990s the number of certified companies had exceeded 100,000, and more than 108 countries had adopted ISO 9000 as their minimum standard for quality. The emergence and growing global acceptance of ISO 9000 conveniently provided a framework for businesses and customers to assess where they were in the quality race and where they needed to be. Certification to ISO 9000 demonstrated a minimum level of acceptable performance that was universally recognized and accepted. However, industrial leaders understood that while ISO 9000 was a very good business process tool, it had some fairly significant shortcomings with regard to product performance and cost improvement. While this shortfall was generally acknowledged, most people still felt it was a very positive first step and proceeded to look upon ISO 9000 certification as a major first step in the quality journey.

In the late 1980s, a number of predominant industry and governmental standards began to feel the "ISO" pressure. Each had developed its own set of expectations, standards, and requirements and were placing a heavy burden on their suppliers not only to comply with the intent of the requirements, but also to fill out the mountains of associated paperwork necessary to demonstrate compliance. The automotive industry leaders (Chrysler, Ford, and General Motors) recognized the burden it was causing with their suppliers. In 1988 the purchasing and supply vice-presidents initiated a task force to create a standard set of manuals, reports, and nomenclature that would apply to the suppliers of the three domestic auto manufacturers. In 1992, the task force set out to create a common assessment system and used the input and support of the major truck manufacturers (Freightliner, Mack Trucks, Navistar International, PACCAR, and Volvo GM Heavy Truck), the International Organization for Standardization, and the Automotive Industry Action Group (AIAG).

In August 1994, QS-9000 was born, and in February 1995, the second edition was released. This standard (improvement tool) incorporates some of the best thoughts that history has to offer. Although it starts with ISO 9000, it adds to it considerably, going well beyond its scope. We believe QS-9000 is the most comprehensive improvement tool available today for manufacturers aspiring to world-class status.

At Span Instruments, we can attest to the dramatic changes QS-9000 has brought. Span is not a current automotive supplier to the Big Three or to the truck industry. We simply chose it for its capability to improve our business. We figured out how to achieve the objectives in 5 $\frac{1}{2}$ months and along the way created a lot of happy customers, employees, and bankers. QS-9000 is just another great tool, and we know from the past, there are better tools coming. It's a never-ending race! The following chapters will describe how the pursuit of QS-9000 is simply good business practice.

1
The Basics

The purpose of this chapter is to familiarize you with QS-9000 and the common sense employed in its design. QS-9000 is the officially recognized common denominator of business and product quality by the automotive industry.

Companies that have been certified to any major quality standard, for example Big 3, ISO 9000, Mil standard, or GMP, are probably more familiar with QS-9000 than they may think. For those who are not familiar with, or are not using these standards, this could be a long journey. But this is not advanced physics or rocket science. It is simply lots of good common sense linked into a single large package. Don't panic, keep going!

WHAT IS QS-9000?

QS-9000 is composed of three modules, each based on established standards affecting the automotive industry and its suppliers as illustrated in Figure 1.1. Each module addresses a different facet of quality as recognized by the Automotive Industry Action Group (AIAG).

Section I: *ISO 9000-Based Requirements*

This section contains an enhanced version of the ISO 9000 standard including 14 extra subsections and an additional 59 major requirements as well as many new "shall" clauses (i.e., mandatory requirements) all designed to incorporate a higher degree of product robustness, process capability, cost controls, and continuous improvement. While they track very closely, the QS version is considerably more prescriptive and

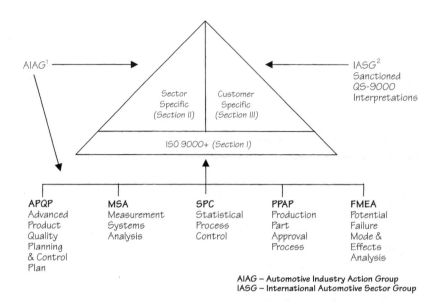

FIGURE 1.1.   Components of the QS-9000 standard.

aggressive in expectation. This module represents the bulk of the QS-9000 standard; however, it relies heavily upon a series of additional standards (reference documents) outside of the basic QS-9000 document itself.

This section is discussed in more detail later in this chapter.

Section II: *Sector-Specific Requirements*

This module is a compilation of common expectations within the automotive industry. These expectations focus on defining three subsections.

1. *The Production Part Approval Process (PPAP).* This process, as outlined in the PPAP document, provides a method by which organizations submit their products to the automotive supplier for acceptance. [The acceptance takes the form of a submission to customer.] The submission should demonstrate how well the product was designed and how well the processes used to make the product performs. The document has a checklist of items organizations must address in their submissions.

2. *Continuous Improvement.* This involves the expectations and techniques for continuous improvement of a company's quality and productivity programs. Organizations must show how they are methodically trying to improve to benefit their customers. Improvements must be in such areas as quality, delivery, lead times, and cost. Organizations also need to identify their planned projects as well as the kinds of methodologies they are using to achieve their improvement goals.

3. *Manufacturing Capability.* This pertains to the minimum expectations for the management and improvement of the manufacturing capabilities within the organization's operations. Companies must show how they are using cross-functional teams to improve and evaluate their manufacturing facilities and processes in conjunction with their quality plans. They must also demonstrate the mistake-proofing techniques they use and explain how they are designing and managing their tools.

Section III: *Customer-Specific Requirements*

The third module represents the areas in which each automotive manufacturer feels it needs its suppliers' undivided attention to its unique critical requirements. Chrysler, Ford, General Motors, and the Truck manufacturers have established their own unique requirements, specifications, references, and contact points. This also includes their requirements with regard to third-party certification. Because of the diversity and uniqueness of each manufacturer, individual organizations must contact each automotive manufacturer and identify those areas that affect that company's products.

SECTION I: ISO 9000-BASED REQUIREMENTS

Why ISO 9000?

During World War II, a series of military standards was born. Later the nuclear industry adopted and built upon them (10cfr series). In the 1970s, the English expanded upon them to encompass the entire business process (BS5750). The International Organization for Standardization (ISO) evolved the British standards to the ISO 9000 standards. The ISO 9000 standards represent the common global denominator of business process quality. It is accepted internationally and was initially adopted in 1987 by the ISO. ISO 9000 certification has come to be recognized as a demonstration of the capability of a supplier to control the processes that determine the acceptability of the product or service being supplied.

By mid-1992 more than 30,000 European companies had been certified, and the numbers were growing dramatically. In contrast, only about 300 U.S. facilities had achieved certification. The Big Three saw what was happening and recognized the benefits standardization would bring to industry and its supplier base. They also saw the power of the tool as it addressed the process side of an operation. In 1994, the ISO 9000 standard was revised and incorporated into the QS standard established in August of 1994. By mid-1996, the global number of ISO 9000 certifications had exceeded 100,000, and Automotive Adaptation QS-9000 was beginning to gain momentum. It is expected that the next revision of the ISO 9000 standard will incorporate elements of QS-9000.

The ISO-Based Elements

The QS-9000 standard utilizes ISO-9000-1 as the reference for its ISO-based requirements. The ISO standard contains 20 elements, each relating to a specific aspect of satisfying customers. Quite often, organizations get lost in all the technical jargon. The best way to decipher the elements is to place yourself in the position of the customer. If you were in their shoes, what would you expect suppliers to do to make sure they met your needs? The following list identifies the 20 elements that begin the QS-9000 standard, providing a brief explanation of each from a customer's perspective.

- *4.1 Management Responsibility.* Who is responsible for ensuring that the product or service is what I ordered and when? Who ensures that your system is effectively managed?
- *4.2 Quality System.* Is the quality system in place to make sure that everything you deliver to me is as you said it would be? How do you make sure?

- *4.3 Contract Review.* What is your system for ensuring that what marketing and sales sold me is what I will actually be getting and when?

- *4.4 Design Control.* Show me how you designed the product and how you make sure it does what you say it does. Is there agreement between the designers and salespeople that it works as they claim? If you make changes to the design, how does everyone determine that my product is still okay? Have you looked at all the ways this product could fail?

- *4.5 Document and Data Control.* How do you inform manufacturing of the requirements and materials for building the product? If you make a change to the requirements, how is that communicated? If I need parts, will you be able to tell me what to order? If changes are made in the material requirements, how is manufacturing informed of how to test it or when to get the new parts in? Will the service organization know the correct parts to bring for a repair job?

- *4.6 Purchasing.* Can you show me how you are making sure that your purchasing group is buying what your designers and engineers are specifying? How do you know you are buying from a supplier who makes good products and delivers them on time?

- *4.7 Control of Customer Supplied Product.* Show me how you protect, store, and maintain the materials I might send you. If there is a problem with the materials, show us how you fix it.

- *4.8 Product Identification and Traceability.* Show me how you make sure my materials don't get mixed up with others and that they are really what you ordered. How do you check that they are what the drawings say they are? How do you make sure they don't use the wrong materials as they are building my product?

- *4.9 Process Control.* Show me that you have procedures in place to build my product properly—I'm especially concerned with procedures on critical items relative to the manufacture of my product. Do you know how to make my product right and can you distinguish between the right way and the wrong way? Do you know when you are making junk? Do you have any places on the product where you cannot tell by inspecting that the product is okay? How do you handle this? The instructions should be written down so that people can easily access them if they have any questions or if they want to train someone.

- *4.10 Inspection and Testing.* How are you ensuring that I am receiving what I ordered? Have you verified that my product will work as promised? I mean really tested—can you show me?

- *4.11 Control of Inspection, Measuring, and Test Equipment.* How do you ensure that the equipment you are using to test the correctness of my product is accurate? How are you doing this?

- *4.12 Inspection and Test Status.* Show me how it is indicated on my product that it was tested.

- *4.13 Control of Nonconforming Product.* Does everyone know what to do when you discover that part of my product doesn't work or fit as it should? Does everyone know what to do even though it is fixed? I would like it to be retested. How do you know it didn't get mixed in with other products after you discovered it wasn't correct?

- *4.14 Corrective and Preventive Action.* If you find a problem with a product, what are you doing to make sure it doesn't happen again? Are you writing new procedures and training people to ensure it doesn't occur again?

- *4.15 Handling, Storage, Packaging, Preservation, and Delivery.* How are you making sure my product was built properly, how are you making sure that it is packaged and stored to prevent damage? Can you make sure the packaging and delivery process keeps my product from being damaged?

- *4.16 Control of Quality Records.* Do you have procedures to document the quality of my product? This should include the raw materials records. Could I find these records quickly if that was our agreement?

- *4.17 Internal Quality Audits.* How are you making sure that you are running your operation as you say? Have you trained a group of people to review your operation? Can you show me records that demonstrate that you are paying attention to the critical areas? Can you show me where the management in the area has fixed a problem discovered by the audit team?

- *4.18 Training.* Prove to me that the people who built and tested my product are trained. Do they know all the critical aspects of my product and how it should work? Has the supervisor agreed that the person is trained properly?

- *4.19 Servicing.* If you told me you could service my product, how will you do that? Can you ensure that you will conduct your operations as well as you did when you first built my product (e.g., good parts, delivered on time, tested again)? Can you ensure that only someone who has been properly trained will work on my product?
- *4.20 Statistical Techniques.* If you are using statistical techniques to validate that my product is good, could you show me that they work? Does everyone who is using these techniques know what to do when they indicate that the process is out of control, or moving outside the control limits?

This brief look at the ISO 9000 components of QS-9000 from a customer's perspective should provide a working approach to the standard. To avoid confusion, just keep asking, what does my customer want?

ISO 9000—An Everyday Example

It is expected that in the not-too-distant future, dealerships, retail repair centers, and basic garages will seek certification to ISO 9000 as the rest of the world has. The following example demonstrates how ISO 9000 could apply to the everyday situation of having your brakes worked on at the local dealership.

You can no longer ignore the screech when you apply the brakes or the effort it takes to get the car to stop. You remember a local dealer's ad for a special on brake repairs; you recall also hearing a neighbor speaking highly of the shop.

As you approach the front counter of the shop, your journey through ISO 9000 begins. The clerk listens to your experience with the brakes as well as about your car. He informs you that your car will require metallic brake pads, which will cost extra. You agree to go ahead with the job, and the clerk promises you your car will be ready in 1 hour.

As you wait, you mull over your main concerns: that the car will stop properly, that the repair won't cost more than they say it will, that they install good quality parts, and that they complete the work in an hour. This is what ISO 9000 is all about—confidence that the task will be done as *promised.*

You realize that when you picked up the advertisement, there was a management structure that made sure the business ran well and that quality methods and practices are used, giving it that good reputation. You want to be confident that the mechanic knows where to get the work order papers for you car, and actually gets *your* car. Hopefully the mechanic has been trained to drive your car onto the ramp properly, disassemble the brakes, and inspect them to ensure nothing else is wrong. Then you want to be assured that the mechanic goes to the proper documents and selects the right brake shoes for your car and retrieves the parts from a bin with the shoes correctly identified. You would expect that if a mechanic tried to use some parts that ended up not fitting, he would have removed them from stock rather than putting them back in and passing the problem on to you. You hope that this person can assemble the brakes to the proper torque requirements and finally test them by driving your car around the block. You expect to be provided with a check-sheet of the items he tested and to know that he parked your car in a safe place. This section with the mechanic covers the 20 ISO 9000 elements (except 4.7), as follows:

- *4.1 Management Responsibility.* Someone is in control ensuring that the organization was selling products and services in the fashion it claims to.
- *4.2 Quality System.* The owners of the operation who indicated they operated their business in a certain way had a quality system in place to ensure it happened. When you approached the counter, the clerk created a contract with you. This person was knowledgeable about the product and communicated with the shop to know approximately how long it would be. The clerk had the training and documents to know that your car required metallic pads, where you should leave your car, and what to do when you came back to pick it up. This person was also willing and able to address your further questions and concerns.
- *4.3 Contract Review.* Ensures that the work that the mechanic was to perform is what you had agreed to with the clerk.
- *4.4 Design Control.* Ensures that the brakes that were being placed on your car were properly designed, tested, and docu-

mented by the manufacturer to ensure that they would perform the job as specified and that the supplier of these parts is reputable and will stand behind them.

- *4.5 Document and Data Control.* Ensures that the documents and reference books were available to the mechanic for the proper selection of materials and the appropriate testing.
- *4.6 Purchasing.* Makes sure that the mechanic had the correct parts available to meet the factory specifications.
- *4.8 Product Identification and Traceability.* Assured that the brake linings were marked properly when they were retrieved from the stock bin. You would also demand that had there been a problem with any part of the brakes, you would be notified and they would be recalled.
- *4.9 Process Control.* There were procedures in place so the mechanic knew how to do the job and fill out the paperwork, knew where to look for information on the materials, and had access to usable assembly instructions.
- *4.10 Inspection and Testing.* The mechanic did some form of inspection and test to ensure that your new brakes were acting properly.
- *4.11 Control of Inspection, Measuring and Test Equipment.* Makes sure that the testing and measurement setting devices are calibrated to the correct torques and the right tools are being used to do it.
- *4.12 Inspection and Test Status.* Ensures that the check-off sheet is really a working document and this person actually tested them.
- *4.13 Control of Nonconforming Product.* Assures that the mechanic knows what to do if he detected some possible problem with the material and how it should be treated and identified after the discovery to prevent it from ending up on the other side of your car.
- *4.14 Corrective and Preventive Action.* Requires that the mechanic and his management have a procedure for fixing known problems, or generally anticipated problems.
- *4.15 Handling, Storage, Packaging, Preservation, and Delivery.* Requires that the mechanic knows how to drive your car, how to handle the brake pads before installation and that they have been

stored in a protected area to assure a long life. Also that he knows where to put your car, keys and paper work when completed.

- *4.16 Control of Quality Records.* The mechanic fills out a standard checklist, makes additional notes on the procedure being performed, and perhaps even has a place to record related issues for your consideration, and for the shop to keep note of.
- *4.17 Internal Quality Audits.* The supervisor should be inspecting throughout the shop regularly to make sure that the mechanic has all the right materials with documents and is doing the job correctly.
- *4.18 Training.* This assures that the mechanic didn't learn on your car and that the supervisor went over the task and verified that the mechanic was successful in all aspects of the job.
- *4.19 Servicing.* Ensures that the mechanic knows what to do if something doesn't work correctly with the new brakes.
- *4.20 Statistical Techniques.* This ensures that metrics are kept regarding the quality of the service provided at the garage and that these are reviewed to ensure that the processes remain in control and that problem areas are quickly identified.

WHY DOES THE STANDARD SEEM SO VAGUE? WHERE CAN I GO FOR MORE INFORMATION?

For those who have the opportunity to read the actual standard, you might very well be saying, "What do they really mean?" Well to begin with, the standard is intentionally vague so it can accommodate just about any business operation. The standard is supported by a wealth of technical documents. If you are the QS-9000 program manager, it is highly unlikely that you will be able to successfully meet this standard without these specific reference documents.

If you are using this book as a stepping stone or as general education tool, the next few chapters will provide you with enough information to understand and comply with the standard. In addition, there are a few key support documents that you will have to become familiar with. Another excellent source of information will come from "IASG Sanctioned

QS-9000 Interpretations." These are available courtesy of Chrysler, Ford, and General Motors. They can be obtained from the IASG.

There is a great deal of misinformation about the standard in the business community, and these interpretations can be very helpful. There are also quite a few ASQC self-help groups springing up daily, and they too can be an excellent source of help, and as always there is the consulting community, which comes with a traditional word of warning. At the time of this writing, approximately 300 sites in the United States are certified, yet there appears to be thousands of consultants claiming QS-9000 expertise—this just doesn't make sense. Although you can't buy certification through a consultant, the best ones can be very helpful in advising you and seeing you through the process. The last word of warning when you do use a consultant, make sure they weave the standard into your organization versus just laying it on top! We will explain more about this concept of "weaving" the standard into your daily operations versus simply putting in another bureaucratic layer.

2
What If We Decide to
_____ Only Become Compliant?

This chapter reviews what QS-9000 means to your operation and describes why you may be required to comply.

GOOD BUSINESS SENSE, EVEN WHEN TIMES ARE GOOD

If your profits are up and business prospects look rosy, you may feel no motivation to change your operations. After all, pain is usually what motivates change. Although you may be leading your market thanks to new technology, you should remember that new technology is also soon-to-be-copied technology, and it's unlikely that you'll enjoy those margins indefinitely. Success is great, but one of its main dangers is complacency. Now may be an ideal time to begin the QS-9000 compliance process. On the other hand, if your firm is experiencing falling sales or profits, QS-9000 may be an effective first step for turning the situation around.

The world has changed—in the 1950s and 1960s a business could operate based on the following formula:

$$\text{Product Cost} + \text{Desired Profit} = \text{Sales Price}.$$

Within reason, you could name your price, and with the appropriate marketing support, you could derive your desired profit. Product cost was not a primary consideration in design or production, and niche

FIGURE 2.1.   Profitability is derived from the combination of sales volume, pricing, and costs.

marketing would support your sales price. The 1990s present an entirely different business climate. Our once attractive formula for business success has been transposed:

$$\text{Sales Price} - \text{Product Cost} = \text{Profit}.$$

Today, markets quickly set and drive prices down, and consumers have difficulty differentiating the performance and quality of competing products. Marketing efforts have mostly saturated consumers. Profit is now often a result of how well you can control and reduce your costs, which historically has been a weak link. Business in the 1990s requires you to employ every effort on total cost reduction. This means more than a purchase price variance on raw materials. It means reducing costs in administration, design, manufacturing—in every corner of your business.

The rest of this chapter examines how QS-9000 can lead to organizational improvements through:

- Growing with the automotive industry.
- Market perception of your company's fitness (both automotive and nonautomotive).
- Internal organizational health.

GROWING WITH THE AUTOMOTIVE INDUSTRY

The Big Three learned the value of the Japanese model of supplier interdependence. Higher internal labor rates and underutilized capacities in the U.S. offer Japanese auto makers a unique opportunity to use suppliers to reduce costs, design products faster, and use their cash in areas more productive than investing in inventories. The increased emphasis on the role of suppliers has created new and unprecedented opportunities. With this opportunity comes a new set of ground rules. Not only will the supplier have to produce a good product at a lower cost, but they will also be required to meet and become certified to QS-9000.

> *"Japanese Car Companies to use QS-9000 in Land Down Under . . . Toyota, Mitsubishi, General Motors, and Ford all have operations in Australia, and with the exception of Toyota, all are requiring their suppliers to be registered by December 1997. Toyota has given its suppliers until June 1998."*
>
> —*Quality Systems Update,* September, 1995

Who's Getting Certified?

Just about anyone who is a direct supplier of production materials to the automotive industry is considered a Tier 1 supplier and is required to comply. According to industry representatives, if you are a direct supplier to Chrysler and General Motors you must be certified in 1997. As of this writing, Ford has not declared a certification date. It has been estimated that there are more than 20,000 Tier 1 suppliers subject to certification requirements.

> *"QS-9000 Affects One in Six Registered Companies According to QSU Survey of ISO 9000 Certified Companies . . . The findings also provide the strongest indication yet that a number of Tier 2 and Tier 3 suppliers will almost certainly be among those companies seeking QS-9000 registration."*
>
> —*Quality Systems Update,* September, 1995

What if My Company Is a Tier 2 or Tier 3 Supplier and We Don't Get Certified?

Certification is not a requirement for Tier 2 or 3 manufacturers at this time; however, compliance is being requested for Tier 2 suppliers, as a result of the standard. All QS-9000 certified and compliant suppliers are required to evaluate their suppliers based on the QS-9000 standard (sections 1 and 2). Tier 1 suppliers can accept a third-party audit of a supplier in lieu of their having to perform one. It is likely that Tier 1 suppliers will encourage Tier 2 and 3 suppliers to become certified, allowing them to avoid an unnecessary expense. If your organization is going to comply with the standard and be evaluated against QS-9000 by Tier 1 customers, it is to your benefit to become certified to avoid the disruptions and extra hidden costs. You might also hear the sales and marketing people suggest that this will improve customer perception of your company!

It has been estimated that there are 30,000 to 45,000 Tier 2 suppliers subject to QS-9000 requirements. It is likely that there are at least as many Tier 3 suppliers. There are a lot of hungry competitors eyeing your business who will stop at nothing to try to win it away. They might even use QS-9000 certification to show your customers that they are better.

> *"QS-9000 Compliance Expected for Secondary Automotive Suppliers . . . It's the next logical step for quality in the automotive industry, stated Raymond J. Mitzel, executive director of the AIAG. In order for Tier 1 suppliers to provide the Big Three with world-class products and services, they must work with quality suppliers all the way down the supply chain."*
>
> —*Quality Systems Update,* April, 1996

Will My Other, Nonautomotive Customers Acknowledge My QS-9000 Certification?

You will probably need to make nonautomotive customers aware of the standard for them to appreciate the full impact of your certification to QS-9000. The good news is that your QS-9000 certificate should state you are also ISO 9000 certified and with that you will be listed in the *Quality Systems Update Directory.*

MARKET PERCEPTION OF YOUR COMPANY'S FITNESS

QS-9000 certification will affect your domestic and international business in at least the following four areas:

- Competitive advantage.
- Continuous improvement.
- Media awareness.
- Customer perception.

Each of these is discussed in the following sections.

Competitive Advantage

Your sales force is trained to capitalize on the strengths of your products and organization. They are also made aware of the competitive issues affecting the organization. Teach your salespeople about QS-9000 certification and explain why you are requiring certification from your suppliers for the parts that go into the products they sell. Arm them with a copy of the certificate, and train them to go out and preach the QS-9000 gospel. You may also want to coach them on how to discuss certification as shown in the following example.

In this example, assume there are two identical brakes (or any identical products), both certified by a reputable laboratory for safety. One brake is manufactured in a QS-9000-compliant environment, meaning the designs are correctly replicated to the manufacturing organization, the approved raw materials are purchased, the product is properly assembled in a robust manufacturing environment by trained employees, tested properly, packaged, transported, and tracked according to procedures. The organization can make incremental improvements in the product because of its stable process and can accommodate all the unique commitments made to you by the customer. The customer has a high probability of receiving the product on time, with a low failure rate, and with an ideal mean-time-between-failure (MTBF).

If the same brake is built in a noncertified facility, it cannot be demonstrated that its designs have been properly replicated by the manufacturing operations, that purchasing was done from a reliable supplier, or that it has been properly assembled by trained employees. There is nothing to show that it was tested properly or to current specifications. There were no guarantees that it was packaged or transported according to procedure. Given this environment, there is a higher probability of late deliveries, higher initial failure rates, and most likely a lower MTBF.

Even though a supplier might have full approval for a product design, it does not necessarily mean the product is manufactured and tested to this design. Formerly, as the manufacturing manager for a company that was just gearing up to become compliant with a government product safety standard, I went to the sales organization for help in identifying the first product to bring into compliance to minimize any potential sales losses. The head salesperson gave me some guidance but assured me that this new law would not affect the company's sales performance or his incentive plan. When I inquired how that was possible, he winked and opened his drawer—out came an entire role of safety stickers that he was placing on the products in his distribution center prior to shipment (yes, I did formally protest!).

In another job as a new director of manufacturing, I decided to spend my second day on the assembly lines meeting the employees and going through the assembly process. This product spent most of its life in dark and damp locations and would accommodate 220 volts. It also carried a Canadian safety sticker. When I got to the end of the assembly line, I noticed that there was no earth-to-ground dielectric test being performed. This test ensures that customers are safe from shock. When I inquired where it had gone, I was told it was a pain to perform and it slowed things down, so my predecessor had removed it. I then asked how they were able to slip this by the visiting inspector. I was told that when he showed up, they told him they weren't building anything for Canada at that time, and he went away (yes, I stopped the line and reinstalled the testing).

If your buyers have a choice between buying from a certified or a noncertified supplier, and they choose the possibly cheaper, noncertified supplier's product, they may well be facing a much grimmer lia-bility situation should the product fail and cause an injury.

Continuous Improvement

In the 1990s, successful organizations share a few key attributes. One of these is speed. This includes the speed of product development, product upgrades and introductions, and even the more mundane func-tions such as responding to a customer inquiry. Speed determines who the profitable leaders are and who the less fortunate followers are.

> *"There is something about speed that transcends its obvious business benefits of greater cash flow, greater profitability, higher share due to greater customer responsiveness, and more capacity from cycle time reductions.*
>
> *Speed exhilarates and energizes. Whether it be fast cars, fast boats, downhill skiing, or business processes. Speed injects fun and excitement into an otherwise routine activity."*

—Jack Welch, General Electric

Speed comes from the repetition of well-defined tasks coupled with the continuous improvement of the supporting operating systems. A competitor who perfects his working quality model before you do will begin to pick up competitive speed, and with speed comes dis-tance. The longer you wait the greater the distance you fall behind your competitors. QS-9000 requires you to define the task of developing methods for continuous improvement.

While the competitor's speed increases, your organization, without the working model, will begin to slow down as you divert resources to brute-forcing results; all the while your resources become further di-minished due to decreasing sales. Soon you are caught in a vicious cy-cle with the only possible solutions being painful ones—if it's not too late altogether.

Here's an example of such a decline. Your sales organization prob-ably has a tough job winning business in a normal environment, where all competitors are on par. If your organization is having difficulties with product quality, response time, or delivery integrity, the first part of your salesperson's call time is usually spent apologizing and sorting out the performance problems before being able to do his sales pitch on the benefits of your products. You are losing a lot of selling time and reducing the effectiveness of sales presentation time. And that's on top of the customer's displeasure with your late delivery, which violates his number-one quality priority and for which he is now personally taking the heat from his management. QS-9000 requires a 100 percent on-time commitment.

If the problem is persistent, your salesperson may never get the chance to sell at all, or worse yet, not meet their sales incentive plan. You can burn through a good sales force quickly, and they will become excellent competitors who know all your weaknesses. It doesn't take long to lose a customer, but it takes quite a bit longer and requires more resources to get those customers back than if you had stabilized your business.

Media Awareness

Achieving QS-9000 is a newsworthy event—especially when most firms don't make it on the first try without the use of a preassessment process—take full advantage of it. Consider the news of your certification just as you would any major event in your company (e.g., a major new product introduction or the appointment of a new senior executive). Get your marketing and communications specialists on-board early (plan on 6 months before certification), educate them, and let them educate the media in your industry and formulate the strategy to maximize the visibility of this landmark achievement. If you're thinking of the costs associated with advertising, think again. Save the money by sending your quality manager to your customers to explain to their quality and materials people how your company became certified. This face-to-face PR will provide your company with much better visibility at only a fraction of the cost. Next, think about further merchandising your achievement by placing your registration mark on your literature, business cards, invoices, and company letterhead. Do not put the registration mark on your product. Certification is a "good housekeeping" seal for your business and in no way infers product fitness (in fact you can lose your certification for such an offense). Also, don't forget to train your sales force on what QS-9000 is and prepare them to answer questions and show the certificate. Did you ever hear of a CEO that didn't want to hear about how to make significant improvements in corporate performance by working with a world-class supplier? Your certification status is also being tracked—recently Dun and Bradstreet ran a series of ads stating that their profiles now contained the ISO 9000 status of a supplier and stated it was a vehicle for improved performance. We suspect that in a very short period of time your QS-9000 status will also be reflected in the profile. A full listing of QS-9000-certified suppliers is maintained by ASQC. Used properly, QS-9000 could make the difference between your sales force gaining access to the executive suite over your competition.

> *"J.D. Powers Predicts Consumer Connection for QS-9000 . . . If the press picks up on this as working for the industry, then I think that it could be promoted in a very effective way to the consumer, the end user . . . Powers sees QS-9000 as having the potential to give the U.S. automobile industry significant leadership gains in the global race for continuous quality improvement."*
>
> —*Quality Systems Update,* June, 1996

Customer Perception

Tom Peters, in his book, *Thriving on Chaos,* describes the results of the PIMS (profit impact of market strategy) study, conducted by the Strategic Planning Institute (Cambridge, MA). This study found that high market share provides profits; however, long-term market share comes from "perceived product or service quality." Perceived means as seen through the customers' eyes rather than the producer's. The study also found that changes in quality have a significantly greater effect on market share than price.

In his book, *Keeping Customers For Life,* James Sewel illustrates how effective the concept of perceived quality can be when coupled with a structured system for customer satisfaction. He presents the results of a study in which a Cadillac dealership with a focus on service and customer perception is compared with Cadillac dealers nationwide.

The measure of the percentage of customers who indicated they would purchase the same model demonstrates how two identical cars can be perceived completely differently.

	One Dealer	Nationwide
Definitely	47%	35%
Probably Not	9%	13%
Definitely Not	3%	9%

It can cost up to five times more to win a new customer than it does to keep an existing one. Sewel's example demonstrates the remarkable advantage this one dealer had over other Cadillac dealers as well as over other manufacturers of similar vehicles. A Gallup poll asked what people were willing to pay for a product that they perceived as having higher than average quality, with the following results:

- Approximately 30 percent more for a better car.
- Approximately 50 percent more for a better household appliance.
- Approximately 200 percent more for a better low-price personal item.

Sewel's results, combined with the Gallup poll, clearly demonstrate the business need to generate high levels of perceived quality for your company and its products. QS-9000 certification offers a clear, readily understandable criterion for evaluation.

A listing of certified facilities in the U.S. and Canada has been compiled by *Quality Systems Update* for ISO 9000, and a directory of certified QS-9000 sites are available from ASQC. As the events and issues associated with QS-9000 unravel, *Quality Systems Update* is an excellent source for learning about the latest developments (800-773-4607).

INTERNAL ORGANIZATIONAL HEALTH

QS-9000 ensures that a foundation for good business practice is in place. It also forces a link between organizations and improves communications. QS-9000 causes a gradual improvement in operations, as it requires implementation of a corrective action process. However, it adds a major competitive advantage in its support of your overall quality improvement program—that is, the profitable growth part. This foundation allows you to meet the challenge of true quality—exceeding your customer's expectations while maintaining profitable growth.

This quality definition can be further broken down to the following seven Ps (you need all seven to consistently exceed your customer's expectations, and the Ps are supported by QS-9000 as well):

1. Product performance to customer's specifications.
2. Perception by customers that needs are exceeded in all areas.
3. Progressive improvement of performance (to meet growing customer expectations).
4. Process stability as a foundation for speed and accuracy.
5. Profitability that allows continued investment and growth.
6. People empowerment (the driving force for meeting customer expectations).
7. Partnership (customers and suppliers).

QS-9000 has far-reaching implications beyond procedures and documentation as illustrated in Figure 2.2. Conformance not only gets an organization onto the global playing field, but it also effects positive organizational change, improves competitive position, enhances the company's market perception, and ultimately improves the bottom line. The choice is yours.

A recent article by McKinsey senior partner Graham Sherman in the *Wall Street Journal* estimates that two of every three quality management programs more than 2 years old are stalled. According to a U.S. General Accounting Office (GAO) study on companies practicing TQM, most quality programs disappear within three years if not supported by senior management.

The purpose of a quality program is not only to create customer satisfaction, but also to eliminate the estimated 20 to 30 percent of the cost of sales that is in non-value-added activities, or waste. If there is no reduction in this waste, it will continue to grow and eventually render your company noncompetitive.

A rule of thumb, according to Arthur Andersen & Co., is that if a typical shop has a lead time of 20 to 40 weeks, it is probable that only 8

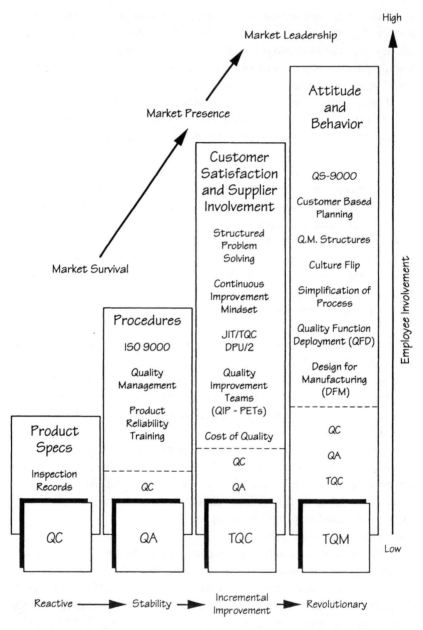

FIGURE 2.2.   QS-9000 certification drives an organization to achieve the highest level of quality evolution.

to 10 hours of processing are required. The rest is dead time, costing you resources and reducing your competitiveness. The shorter the lead time, the more competitive your business. This is true in all aspects of your business. For example, according to a recent *BusinessWeek* study of business operations, researchers within companies spend less than 20 percent of their day doing research. The rest is spent on things like staff meetings, writing reports, or ordering supplies. Spending more time on their primary task would reduce their lead times and hopefully result in faster new product developments and better designs.

A study conducted by quality guru Bill Conway on the amount of approximate time people spend working found that:

- More than 25 percent of the time people aren't working (vacations, holidays, and breaks).
- More than 40 percent is unnecessary work.
- Only 35 percent is necessary work and is adding value.

The bottom line is that your organization needs to be continually structuring for improved speed while restructuring to focus on niche opportunities. Although these two statements seem incongruous, they support each other very nicely. At the heart of the business should be systems that are well rehearsed and where variations can be eliminated. According to Japanese quality guru Tagucchi, the more you reduce variation and center your processes, the better your product or service will be. He poses the question, "What is the real difference between a product that barely makes the specification versus one that barely misses?" As with most things in life, and with all repetitive events, moving up the learning curve results in speed and accuracy. Further refinement results in reduced resource requirements as your rework goes down. This reduction in resources needed to operate your core business makes resources available to focus on continued improvement of the process. There is an old acronym that aptly defines the concept of TIME as it relates to quality, that is, "Time Is My Enemy." The longer it takes to detect a problem, the more the waste that is produced. The slower you are at resolving the problem, the more you have to fix later. The slower you are at introducing a new product, the greater the probability that someone else will do it before you. As Tom Peters states in *Thriving on Chaos,* "If you are not reconfiguring your organization to become a fast-changing, high-value-adding creator of niche markets, you are simply out of step." The PIMS study found that firms who scored in the top third of the Perceived Product Quality index out-earned those in the bottom by a two-to-one margin. A study was conducted by the GAO, from June 1990 through February 1991, on the effects of total quality management. It studied 20 companies that were practicing TQM and looked at what occurred in these companies as they were pursuing TQM. The GAO focused on the following areas with the averaged results achieved by these companies:

- Market share improvement: 13.7%
- Customer complaints down: 11.6%
- Order processing times down: 12.0%
- Defects declined: 10.3%
- Turnover down: 6.0%
- Suggestions up: 16.6%
- Employee relations improved by a ratio of 4.3 to 1
- Operating indicators posted positively with 90 percent of the companies surveyed.

A further breakdown of these indicators reveals the following:

Manufacturing	% Reporting Favorable Improvement	Average % Improvement
Reliability	100%	11.3%
Delivery	89%	4.7%
Order Process Time	100%	12.0%
Errors or Defects	88%	10.3%
Lead Times	86%	5.8%
Inventory Turns	67%	7.2%
Cost of Quality	100%	9.0%
Cost Savings	100%	
Customer Service		
Customer Satisfaction	86%	2.5%
Customer Complaints	83%	11.6%
Customer Retention	40%	1.0%

Financial Return	% Reporting Favorable Improvement	Average % Improvement
Market Share	82%	13.7%
Sales Per Employee	100%	8.6%
Returns on Assets	77%	1.3%
Return on Sales	75%	4.0%

It should be noted that those firms that saw a decline in the financials cited foreign competition and indicated that TQM strategies reduced the decline in economic performance. Overall the financial ratios improved in 87 percent of companies reporting. In addition, the greater the belief in the financial return, the greater the investment in TQM. Florida Power and Light Company (FP&L) determined that for every dollar invested in their TQM program, they achieved a return of four dollars.

A commonly asked question by senior management is, "How does QS-9000 compare to ISO 9000, the Baldrige criteria, and the Shingo award?" ISO 9000 focuses very closely on internal processes, especially manufacturing, sales, administration, and technical support and services. The Baldrige places more emphasis on customer satisfaction and business results. QS-9000 is somewhere in the middle: it uses ISO 9000 but aggressively addresses product performance while embracing the techniques that support customer satisfaction. Some would argue that QS-9000's emphasis on continuous improvement and link to productivity provide for a comfortable step into the Shingo improvement tool, which looks strongly at productivity.

The Shingo Prize (or tool) is a relatively new tool in the quality improvement bag and has been growing rapidly in popularity. It was established in 1988 and is administered by the Utah State University, College of Business at Logan. The award is given annually to manufacturers who exhibit world-class manufacturing leadership. The sections of the Shingo Prize are illustrated in Figure 2.5.

Like the Baldrige, the Shingo Prize requirements assume that processes are under control: the Shingo, however, places a high emphasis on productivity improvements, as does QS-9000. It is projected that as a manufacturer achieves QS-9000 compliance, the Shingo would become a logical extension as a tool for improvement. The following are some commonly asked questions related to ISO 9000, QS-9000, and the Malcolm Baldrige National Quality Award.

Should We Go for the Baldrige Award or ISO 9000 Certification or QS-9000 First?

If you are not required to be immediately QS-9000-compliant, go for ISO 9000 compliance first. Achieving certification can help you prepare for the QS-9000 upgrade and will act as a pathway to the Baldrige. The applications for the Baldrige Award have decreased since its inception. It was felt by the Baldrige committee that this was in response to companies going for ISO 9000 certification first, state quality awards based upon the Baldrige Award, and those pursuing the Shingo Prize.

What's the Difference Between ISO 9000, QS-9000, the Shingo, and the Baldrige Award?

ISO focuses very closely on internal processes, especially manufacturing, sales, administration, and technical support and services as seen in Figure 2.3. QS-9000 adds to ISO 9000 and makes a process and product more robust, illustrated in Figure 2.4. The Shingo builds on QS-9000 and focuses on productivity and improvement as seen in Figure 2.5. The Baldrige places more emphasis on customer satisfaction and business results, as illustrated in Figure 2.6.

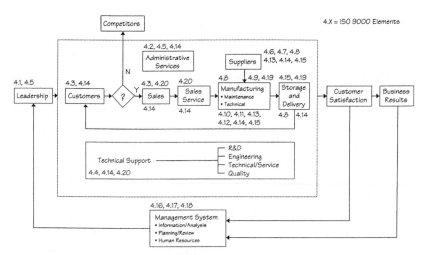

FIGURE 2.3.   ISO 9000 emphasis areas. (Source: Weyerhauser Company)

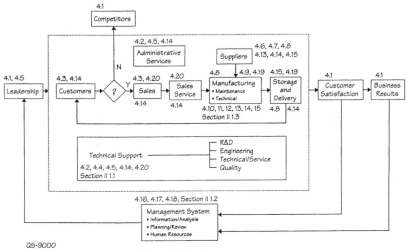

QS-9000
Section I: 4.X = ISO 9000 Elements plus 14 additional subsections and 59 additional requirements
Section II: Production part approval, continuous improvement, manufacturing capability
Section III: Customer based requirements, can affect all areas

FIGURE 2.4.   QS-9000 emphasis areas.

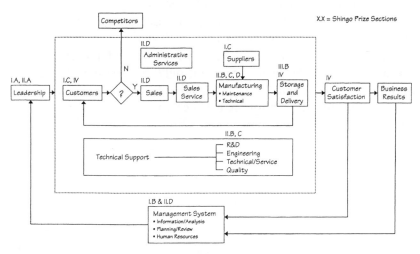

FIGURE 2.5.   Shingo Prize emphasis areas.

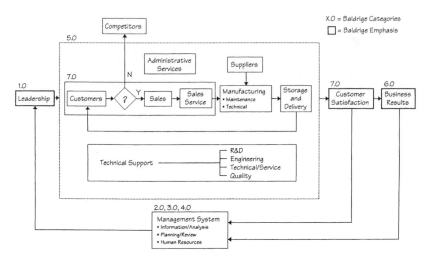

FIGURE 2.6.   Baldrige Award emphasis areas.

Do You Have to Be Certified to ISO 9000 or QS-9000 Before Going for the Baldrige or Shingo?

The Baldrige and Shingo assumes your processes and products are under control and therefore awards relatively few points in this area. The Baldrige addresses the issues of customer satisfaction, business results, and the competitive aspects of gaining increased sales and profitability. ISO 9000 virtually ignores competitive positioning.

QS-9000 has far-reaching implications beyond procedures and documentation. Conformance will not only get you onto the global playing field, but it will also effect positive organizational change, improve your competitive position, enhance your company's market perception, and ultimately improve your bottom line.

3
Preparing for QS-9000

For most companies, QS-9000 certification either augments ongoing quality efforts or sparks a renewed emphasis on quality, a win in either case. The big questions in a lot of executives' minds are, "How can I get it?," "How quickly?," and "How much will it cost me?" This chapter describes the background and motives behind Span Instruments' QS-9000 undertaking. This effort was unique, not because Span is certified to QS-9000 and does not produce automotive products, but due to the speed with which a foreign standard was integrated into the operations. Span was not required by a customer to become certified; rather it was looking for a tool that would allow the organization to quickly move to a reasonable state of operational quality. QS-9000 had all the attributes needed to make this a reality, and management understood the rewards of such an endeavor. While not immediately subject to certification, there was the future possibility that Span could be selling a few products to the Big Three automotive makers. Span's mainstream products could potentially fall within a Tier 3 supplier status within the tooling and equipment arena. Its pressure measurement products are used extensively by the semiconductor manufacturing industry. There is approximately $5 billion in annual semiconductor sales to the automotive industry, and these products and their manufacturers are considered part of the Tier I supplier group and are subject to certification.

Span Instruments, located in Plano, Texas, develops, manufactures, engineers, and integrates pressure measurement instruments and sensing devices for the semi-conductor and high purity industries. Span is a medium-sized company with approximately 400 people and has become a member of the Tylan General Corporation.

Span, a privately held company, has been in existence for more than 20 years and has undergone dramatic and uncontrolled growth over the past few years. To accommodate this growth, an aggressive expansion program had been put in place; however, the infrastructure and operational practices failed to keep up with the demand, and the company was suffering. The dramatic growth in manufacturing capacity and facility needs had placed a tremendous strain on cash flow, while poor business processes were wiping out what should have been reasonable margins. Product quality and delivery integrity were poor, and lead times had stretched to four times that of the competition. Product developments were late, and documentation and manufacturing practices varied greatly. To further compound an already tenuous situation, because of the cash squeeze, suppliers were being stretched to the point that a significant portion of the material was coming in COD. This was further complicating a struggling and poorly defined manufacturing process. The net result was that the dominant market position Span had enjoyed was in jeopardy as upstart competitors were growing in the vacuum created by Span's loss of process integrity and ability to keep up with market growth. Unless Span was able to pull out of its tailspin, the future economic viability of the company was in question.

A few years ago a cartoon by Gary Larson of *The Far Side* described Span's situation. It pictured a dinosaur behind a podium addressing a conference of dinosaurs, with the caption, "The picture's pretty bleak, gentlemen ... The world's climates are changing, the mammals are taking over, and we all have a brain about the size of a walnut." Span was experiencing the same dramatic change. Unless it began to focus and use its intelligence, Span would have suffered the same fate.

The owners made a decision to replace the existing management that had twice failed to launch an ISO 9000 effort, and during the summer of 1995 an entirely new team was pulled together with the goal of pulling the operation out of its tailspin. The first task was to align material flows, stabilize throughput capabilities, and firm up minimal quality practices, while developing a plan for conversion to a world-class manufacturing operation and putting in place the resources to launch it down the path.

SPAN'S EVOLUTION TO WORLD-CLASS MANUFACTURING

In 1987, the Touche Ross consulting group released a study that identified the factors critical for a company to achieve world-class status. The group benchmarked various automation suppliers to determine the critical factors for success. The results of the study indicated that Span would need to embrace the following principles if it were to survive:

- There is no safe harbor from the onslaught of competition—we were already witnessing the wave of local and Japanese competition. The reality is, no industry is secure, and our management had to address a mind-set that embraced change and learn to rapidly respond to it.
- Thresholds for performance continually increase. The strong capabilities of today become the mediocre performances of tomorrow. Process capabilities must improve, and speed determines the winners.
- The leaders in the market dictate the standards. If we can hold the lead, we can set the standards that would cause our competitors to follow. If you aren't the leader, your profits will reflect your "me too" status.
- To remain viable you must always attempt to exceed the new standards, realizing that it takes time to get there, and by the time you do achieve your goal, the standard probably will have grown to meet your improvement.
- Quality is the number-one requirement for customer satisfaction in the 1990s and beyond. It will become a minimum checkpoint.
- Quality is to be defined by our customers, regardless of what we believe. Our customers will point the way. Those companies that are able to maintain a close relationship with their customers will gain the greatest understanding of their requirements, and in turn, will have the opportunity to produce the best product for the customer first. Those companies that are able to demonstrate conformance to their customers' standards will enjoy market share.

We now believe that QS-9000 certification is one of the many conformance standards that Touche Ross was foretelling. The management team also studied other success models such as that of General Electric, where speed and cross-functional teams are a way of life.

Span's program included many of the concepts found in Richard J. Schonberger's book, *World-Class Manufacturing.* We recognized that most of these concepts were not new and, in fact, can be traced back to Henry Ford. The program also adopted the teachings of other leaders like Juran, Morgensen, Feigenbaum, and a host of contemporary Japanese experts.

The management team began the process by developing a priority list of customer expectations. We visited our top three customers who represented most of our market and listened to their expectations of suppliers. Their expectations are discussed in the following sections.

Customer Requirements

Product Quality.

Our customers wanted us to reduce our product performance variability and consider the product specification as a minimum baseline. They also felt that the defect rates of the past were no longer acceptable. Customers warned that sellers of products that couldn't perform better than at a 5000 ppm warranty period defect rate would no longer be considered viable contenders for their business. Our largest customers showed us the importance of product variability and how it impacts their operations. Delivering a product to specification was no longer good enough; we had to reduce the variability within the specification.

Delivery Integrity.

This was the most important measure of quality as expressed by our customers' buyers. Buyers are driven by two major factors: Did the product arrive on time? and What is my purchase price variance? We realized we could never get beyond the buyers to sell our products if we did not perform on the first measure, and it was apparent that we could not keep apologizing much longer.

Process Integrity.

Our customers understand that if our processes exhibit a high level of process integrity (control), they are far more likely to receive a good product, on time, at the lowest total cost to them. In fact, our customers pointed out that we could not consistently deliver any of their requirements unless we had our processes under control. For them, certification to ISO 9000 was just the beginning of demonstrating that our processes were under control. Their audits of us were based on ISO 9000 but continued beyond it to include their specific product concerns; they were beginning to feel like QS-9000 audits. Without process integrity, our customers realized they could not rely on our efforts, and all our other remedies would therefore be in vain.

Reduce Lead Times.

Our customers wanted us to figure out a way to deliver small quantities quickly. Last-minute changes to their orders often dictate quicker responses. This is critical to our distributors, because even though they stock products, they undergo surges and wanes. The more we make them wait, the more they have to stock, which incurs cost and blinded us from what the market was really doing. These excessive distributor and customer stocks driven by long lead times would only exacerbate our manufacturing adjustment difficulties when a downturn would eventually occur. This cost is borne by the end users, or worse, enjoyed by the competition.

Increase Flexibility.

This is the improved ability to call out various configurations in modular combinations. Our customers also spoke of flexibility in terms of delivery crisis and unique product design opportunities. One of our customers had experienced a major production line shutdown, and they were quoting a loss of $1 million per day. The supplier who could respond the fastest with the right pieces of equipment would win their business. It was therefore a requirement to put strategic inventory in locations where Span could support 100+ pieces of a unique product and literally have it ready overnight. Our customers let us know that they depend on that kind of capability.

Administration and Technical Support.

One customer was looking at the total cost of doing business and realized that the purchase price was usually a small fraction of the total cost of ownership. Part of the cost was correctness of paperwork along with getting answers back to them.

The example used to make this point was that of returning quotes promptly. They were sometimes not as interested in a firm delivery date as they were in knowing whether they could get the part in the configuration they required to support the application. If one supplier couldn't answer the question, they would have to move on to another competitor until they could find someone who could. Another customer had a system where if there were ever any questions about the product (good, bad, or questionable), they would remove it immediately from their process and call it defective. Suppliers had 5 days to address the problem and provide them with an analysis of it; if no defect was found, the supplier would avoid a "quality ding." Initially, Span dealt with a distributor and was unaware of this program and therefore was responding to the distributor's return within the normal 30 days. Span determined that using distributors no longer made good business sense and ceased using them to service our customers. In this case, we were immediately faced with the challenge of administering this response process. We also found out that our customers were very upset about our quality performance. Their data indicated that we were suffering from a 30,000-ppm defect rate. Our own sampling systems said we were below that number by a factor of 10+. When we began to administer the response effort, we quickly realized that our customer's installation people were poorly informed about our product configurations, applications, and characteristics. In the first 3 months of a direct relationship and addressing the administrative aspects, our customers experienced a 0-ppm defect level. Span had made some improvements to its product integrity, but the vast majority came from simply watching the administrative response process.

We had learned a similar lesson with a previous employer with regard to order acknowledgments and product markings. The customer pointed out that even though our instrument price was less than our competitor's, when the customer received the instrument and couldn't match it with its order paperwork, they spent $130 trying to reconcile the two, making the instrument more expensive. We were also told that if we could put the customer's inventory location and routing instructions on the upper right-hand corner of the box, we could reduce their cost by $30, making the instrument much less expensive than our competitor's. Not enabling our customers to easily match our invoices with the material received frustrates their receiving operations, which is usually tied into the materials organizations (where the buyers are located). When they can't receive material easily, they have a tendency not to pay very quickly, which then puts pressure on your receivables department, which in turn, further harasses the customer for prompt payment. The result? Your relationship with your customer deteriorates rapidly.

New and Improved Products that Support the Lowest Life-Cycle Cost.

If we can invest in a product component that extends the mean time between failure from 15 years to 30, we will do it. If we can produce a device that requires calibration only once a year instead of twice, we will go ahead with the improvement, even if it does cost significantly more. Otherwise our customer would have to bear the cost of sending out a crew to calibrate or replace the instrument or possibly shut down an operation generating revenue at a rate of thousands of dollars per minute. Our customers are becoming very astute on the issue of total cost, realizing that the purchase price of a product is just a fraction of the total cost of a product.

Concurrent Development.

Our customers have unique competitive opportunities with limited windows to capture market share. A good supplier will move quickly with its customers to help them capture the opportunity and will develop a structured ongoing relationship that will support their customers' needs. Our customers were asking us to help them become more competitive—that's what it's all about. You won't be successful if your people don't know their roles and the system remains undefined. QS-9000 compliance addresses these two factors. Supporting these defined customer needs required us to restructure the way we planned and carried out our business.

Gaining Control

Our employees were already at full tilt attempting to make an inadequate system perform. Fire-fighting was the order of the day, and it was tough to hear anything over the roar of quality, materials, and delivery problems. In addition, we had been through two prior failed ISO 9000 drives, and while everyone was eager for a change, most people were somewhat doubtful that we would ever get certified. Employees had more priorities than they could handle and had eventually settled on addressing either the problems they felt they could control or areas where the screaming was the loudest.

Senior management determined that to overcome the inertia in place, they would focus what remaining energies were available on the installation of QS-9000. There would be no additional major projects, and the company's resources would be exclusively directed toward on-time delivery, product quality, and implementing the ISO/QS-9000 tool. Employees needed to have a few clear priorities, so an ISO/QS-9000 team was formed to work on the development effort and an ISO/QS-9000 quality documentation control position was established. This position also served as the control point for all data regarding overall business performance. The team included a key supervisor from each operational area. Their duties were to operate their departments while delivering their areas into an ISO/QS-9000 compliant position. The ISO/QS-9000 challenge became their primary project.

We realized the faster we could cause the organization to understand the QS-9000 tool, the more comfortable they would become and the more quickly they would make full use of the tool. From this need, we developed the concept of high-velocity learning (HVL) illustrated in Figure 3.1.

HVL is based partially on Deming's profound knowledge concept of learning. It calls for an initial study of, the task, going out and performing the task, and then comparing what had been studied with what actually happened. Doing the comparison would result in learning. Our situation and the anxiety created by undertaking this goal further contributed to the learning process.

The concept was to allow the organization to see the benefits of the QS-9000 tool and its components, including both the competitive pitfalls for not meeting this goal as well as the positive impact it could

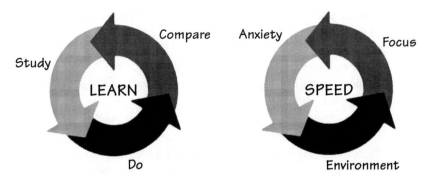

FIGURE 3.1. High-velocity learning at Span.

have on their lives. This technique would reinforce management's commitment and remind them that they didn't want to be the ones who would cause the organization to fail. When the president and the senior management commit to and act in a fashion consistent with their goals, it gets the attention of the employees, and their anxiety begins to rise out of a desire to avoid failing as well as the need for a positive change.

Once the organization's anxiety is heightened, it is then management's job to focus on a few achievable milestones. As the organization focuses on and achieves the key milestones, progress is made, positive feedback is provided, and the organization's confidence grows. As each milestone is met, renewed confidence and consistent anxiety diminish any hesitation that might occur. The milestones should be as serial as possible.

The last key element to HVL is simply the environment. Management must create an environment where what is learned is practiced regularly. In this case, management must continually embrace the QS-9000 structures and ensure that their people live it.

To summarize, educate employees quickly, focus them on a few activities that will install the tools they need, and then have them utilize the tools.

Minimizing Cultural Resistance

The move to QS-9000 required a sizable shift in behaviors for our culture. Management knew that a cultural shift was needed and used Juran's concepts to minimize resistance:

- *Provide participation.* Try to involve all the affected parties and allow them a voice into the change.
- *No surprises.* Ensure the affected organizations and members know of the plan, their roles, and its timing.
- *Provide enough time.* Allow adequate time for proper planning and organization.
- *Create a favorable social climate.* Keep the event friendly and ensure that the members are recognized for their contributions. Bring them together as a team that is on the path to succeed.
- *Start small.* Set achievable goals in the beginning, with clear milestones for success. Prototype and have the members affected try out the prototype and gain confidence before they initiate widespread change.
- *Weave the change into something that is already accepted.* Try to use that which is already working well and accepted. If an organization already has a procedure format, use it or modify it. Don't toss it out just because your group didn't invent it. Weave the QS-9000 standard into the organization using what is already working and then upgrade. Very rarely have we witnessed processes or procedures that needed to be tossed outright. Instead, they can be generally modified or upgraded to meet the intended requirements.

The team continued looking to the visionaries and incorporated their messages. While it may seem that the team spent a considerable effort understanding the human side of the transition, they realized it was the people and the culture that would determine our eventual success. We have also learned that a good plan and understanding of the event is well worth the effort in both time and resources. Without a well-thought-out plan communicated, the organization would lose an opportunity for rapid project execution and waste its precious few resources.

ELEMENTS OF WORLD-CLASS MANUFACTURING

We identified five strategic components and subsets that supported the rapid transition to our long-term goal of world-class manufacturing

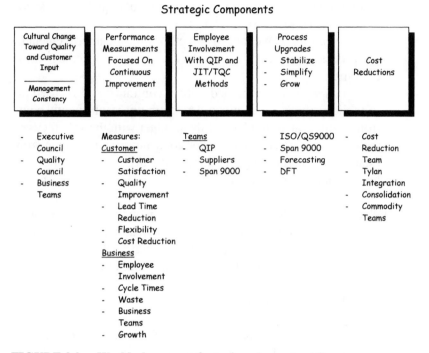

FIGURE 3.2.   World-class manufacturing elements at Span.

(see Figure 3.2). QS-9000 certification was just a milestone along the way. These components were:

- *A cultural change toward quality.* There needed to be a constancy of management, where all the managers practiced a common form of continuous improvement over a sustained period of time. This constancy would come from the executive council, quality council, and the business teams.
- *Performance measures focused on continuous improvements.* We needed to establish measures that allowed us to calibrate our rate of improvement in those areas that were critical to both the customers and the overall health of the business and stakeholders.
- *Employee involvement with quality improvement, just in time, and total quality methods.* It would be necessary to have everyone

participating in our efforts to improve the total quality and speed of process and response.

- *Process upgrades.* We looked at methods for the improvement of our processes, methods for product design, and listening to the customer.
- *Cost reduction.* There needed to be a continued and focused effort to identify cost reductions. The optimum results would come from teams that would look at the product with the sole focus of taking costs out. The other major contributor would come from establishing purchasing commodity teams, which would also look for a total cost reduction.

With our customer's voice ringing loudly in our ears and a vision of what was required to make a world-class organization, we set a world-class manufacturing plan in motion. Our strategy called for three sequential phases: stabilize, simplify, and grow as seen in Figure 3.3.

Phase I: Stabilize the Operation

This phase called for us to use tools that would cause the business to define and measure itself. Where we found inconsistencies or holes, structures would be put in place to gain control of the process, respond to customers, and gain a handhold on the suppliers. Speed was the operative word, where cost could be reduced quickly, resources would be deployed. It was not intended to develop the optimal system; the goal was to simply install a good working foundation that would support future activities. This definition would entail a detailing of charters and responsibilities along with the tools and documents needed to communicate and follow up. At the end of this phase we would have an organization that was sound operationally and financially, but not optimized. The following were the components of phase I:

- Use ISO/QS-9000 procedures/linkages/training.
- Initiate SPC/precontrol processes.
- Develop product and business measures.
- Introduce the Span 9000 product development process.
- Develop and adhere to a standard corrective action process.
- Establish a quality assurance function for returns.

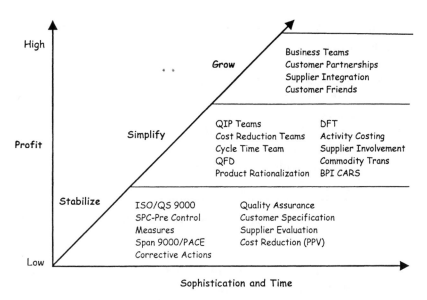

FIGURE 3.3.   Three steps to achieving total business quality: stabilize, simplify, grow.

- Work with customer-driven specifications.
- Initiate a supplier evaluation process.
- Work at cost reduction at PPV and avoidance.

At the top of the plan was the call to use ISO/QS-9000 as the tool that would support definition of our business operations as well as our roles and responsibilities. By using the QS-9000 standard we would be addressing the entire phase I. The certification to QS-9000 represented the milestone marker for phase I completion.

Phase II: Simplify

Once the organization was defined and operational, the force of all the employees would be brought online to begin the systematic process of removing the non-value-added work from the operations. This represented incremental improvements in time, cost, steps, and accuracy of the operations' activities. It would build upon the systems put in place during phase I. All the employees are involved in some form of improvement activity. The elements of phase II included:

- Quality improvement process teams for problem solving.
- Cost reduction teams.
- Cycle time teams (JIT/TQC).
- Quality function deployment (QFD).
- Product rationalization.
- Demand flow technology (DFT).
- Activity costing.
- Supplier involvement with commodity teams.
- Business process improvement, customer action requests (BPI CARS).

The net effect of phase II would be a reduction in the resources required to run the operation and thus freeing resources for phase III development as well as rewarding the stakeholders for their patience.

Phase III: Grow

With a stable vertical organization that is becoming leaner and more efficient, freeing up both capital and human talent, the organization then establishes a series of horizontal business teams. Each team draws upon the resources and human talent freed up and focuses on a product line and determines how to double the business in a defined period. This same team then works with the vertical organization to deploy resources to accomplish the doubling of the size, market share, or profits of that particular business.

With the plan mapped out and groups educated, we began a 14-step program to support the QS-9000 certification as described in Chapter 4.

4
The Fast Track to QS-9000

Qualifying for and receiving certification is an enterprise-wide endeavor. Even with management commitment and an existing quality infrastructure in place, it can take anywhere from 3 to 18 months to mobilize your operations and get the proper documents, procedures, internal audits, and practices in place. This chapter describes the events leading up to a certification audit, based on the experiences at Span Instruments.

HOW LONG WILL IT TAKE?

The following time frames for certification are suggested; they assume a single plant operation and management commitment:

- 3 to 6 months—If you are in compliance to a military standard, nuclear, ISO 9000 standard, or a Big Three Automotive Certification.
- 6 to 12 month—If your organization has fairly up-to-date procedures, job descriptions, and a working quality organization.
- 12 to 18 months—If the organization has only sketchy procedures and its records are haphazard or if you don't know what an APQP or PPAP is. Your quality organization is still responsible for final inspection and still takes the blame for the substandard product shipped. Or if you have a very large plant site.
- 18 to 24 months—If you still don't have full commitment from senior management. You shouldn't begin your countdown until management commits to pursuing certification.

Most operations are focused on immediate problems, such as sales and profits (and little else counts). Our survey of companies who achieved QS-9000 early indicates that until there is a "stake in the ground" (i.e., a target date set for certification) and people can see it coming, little motivation exists to work toward it. Such an experience can be very frustrating for those trying to generate any meaningful effort.

HOW MUCH WILL IT COST?

The cost of QS-9000 compliance depends on the existing condition of your organization. Most certified companies have not tracked the costs. As discussed earlier, the value to the business far outweighs the cost, so tracking these costs is a non-value-added activity as long as your operation stays within its planned operating budget. In a series of comparable ISO 9000 studies, the average payback period became a function of size, with the average running between 1 and 2 years. The study was based on a general postcertification questionnaire, where the opportunity costs were not captured. In another study of one company where the project was tracked from the very beginning, the postaudit study showed a nine-month return on investment. Again it is a function of your current status, but the greater the opportunity for improvement, the greater the opportunity for return.

When Span's managers were first told of the plan for the upgrade to QS-9000 it was not widely welcomed. Span had unsuccessfully tried to achieve ISO 9000 certification two times with prior management teams and QS-9000 was even more difficult. The new president addressed this issue by assuring that certification was one of his top five personal goals and made sure his staff stayed focused on his goals. It was also becoming apparent that we needed the basic ISO certification just to stay competitive. We also understood that QS-9000 addressed all the issues that go along with running a good business, the things we were supposed to be doing all along!

The management team laid out a plan, the president made it part of his plan, and we were off. The next section describes the 14 steps that will enable you to measure your progress and estimate when you will be able to entertain the auditors with a world-class operation that is fully compliant with QS-9000.

THE 14 STEPS

The following sections describe the process Span used to quickly achieve compliance and certification. This is just one approach; individual organizations should try to create plans tailored to their specific situations.

Step 1: Senior Management Commits

The old adage that commitment must come from the top holds true. Senior management must demonstrate their commitment to achieving QS-9000 compliance by allocating the necessary resources and assigning responsibility appropriately. QS-9000 is an enterprisewide standard that requires the shared commitment and involvement of all the executives within the senior management group and their respective operations. Remember this is not a free lunch; sacrifice is required for this commitment. Your organization has two choices, it can fund an outside consultant with a staff of writers, or it can slow other projects down and perform the task with internal people who are close to the process and can usually do a much better job than any outsider. If you decide to go internally, your management must keep in mind that this is not business as usual; a strong commitment is needed.

At Span, our employees and supervisors determined what would slow down. As long as it did not interfere with delivery integrity or functional quality, their recommendation was generally accepted. The only requirement was to let us know what the impact would be.

Once you have senior management commitment, actively use it. Ask your plant managers to put QS-9000 at the top of each staff meeting. This way it will not get lost in the agenda, and putting it first will send a clear message to the staff. Declare your intentions throughout the entire organization with a letter of commitment from the senior person in the organization. The commitment will serve you well, and without it, your chances for success are significantly reduced.

Step 2: Establish a QS-9000 Steering Council

The primary charter of this council is to establish a comprehensive QS-9000 development program and ensure its implementation with the proper allocation of resources. This group acts as the focal point for all the activities within the organization related to QS-9000. They will provide the comprehensive assessments necessary for scheduling and supporting the audit. They will be negotiating tasks and interfaces within their own organization in their role as the project leaders, as well as between organizations for linkages (the toughest part).

Recognize that QS-9000 is an enterprisewide effort when putting this council together and that everyone must be involved. As you are preparing for QS-9000, be sure to include representatives from all organizations that are involved in areas affected by certification. When you go to senior management for representatives, ask for the best. Remind them that these people will be representing them and committing their organizations to plans of action. Remind them that they do not want to be the organizational group that causes the company to fail (that reminder seems to be effective in areas that are not completely committed). Make sure the people assigned to the committee are your best performers. Although it seems that they can't be spared for the task, you need the best. Once they are on the team, remind their managers that this is not a free ride—they should work with their designate to free up some of his or her time and see that they receive recognition for this work. With the good performers on your team, you will notice that they receive peer support that will make accomplishment of the overall mission easier. One of the first tasks should be the education of the council.

> **Tip—Organization:** We broke the Quality effort down into three distinct functions: Quality Control (QC), Quality Assurance (QA), and Total Business Quality (TBQ).
>
> The Quality Control group addresses activities associated with the conformance of the operations to the processes defined and requirements of the products. This oversight includes all inspections, sampling, calibration, and control of measurement devices and the Measurement System Analysis supporting the measurement and testing needed to evaluate the re-

quirements of the product. This group also provides oversight of the QS-9000 effort and the organization's conformance to the standard. This includes the Internal Audits of the Operations as well as the maintenance of the Corrective Action Process. In addition, this group provides documentation control over the procedures and work instructions along with the maintenance of the Quality Records.

The Quality Assurance operations focus on the performance of the product from a customer's perspective. This group ensures the product meets or exceeds the specifications defined. They provide an analysis and corrective action response for products that fail in and out of warranty. They work with engineering, manufacturing, and QC to address these product shortfalls.

The Total Business Quality Function works with the customers and organization to initiate a series of continuous improvement activities and to collect measures reflective of stakeholder needs.

These three groups became the major force in facilitating and driving the QS-9000 effort.

Step 3: Educate the Council on QS-9000 and Establish Performance Measures

It is critical that the council members understand QS-9000 and its associated documents such as the Production Part Approval Process (PPAP) and the Advanced Product Quality Planning and Control Plan (APQP) to a reasonable level of detail, as they will champion the effort in their respective organizations. It is also important that they reach a common agreement on which aspects of QS-9000 are within their own organization. To start this effort, obtain a copy of the QSA (Quality System Assessment) from the Automotive Industry Action Group (AIAG). We suggest you convert them to your language and use them as a key element in your education and organizational readiness assessment process. The education of the steering committee creates a group of roving experts, who are also self-reinforcing drivers with the ability to move the process forward quickly. People generally don't want to put work into something when they don't understand the reasoning behind it. If your team can convey the purpose of the effort and provide correct and timely answers to questions, they will motivate the other employees to join the effort.

Once the team becomes familiar with the requirements, they should consider establishing milestone measures that reflect the progress of the project. Try to keep these measures simple and easy to collect, ensure clear ownership, and make sure senior management understands and sees them regularly. Here are a few of the measures you might want to consider:

- How many work instructions and procedures will we have to write and control.
- How many work instructions and control plans will we have to fix (postaudit).
- The number of QCARs needed to be closed.
- The percentage of training records completed.
- The percentage of job descriptions completed.
- How many more departments have to be audited.

Step 4: Evaluate and Select an Accredited Registrar

Due to the impending demand for third-party audits and the limited number of third-party certifying auditors, we suggest that you not delay this selection process. The evaluation and selection of a registrar is critical and should be viewed as a marriage between two parties. The following is a checklist of things to consider when you search for a registrar:

- Your certification audit should not be the first time you meet your auditors. Plan on spending some time selecting your registrar (i.e., check references, cost, and ability).
- Does this registrar carry a recognized European registration mark for ISO 9000 as well as QS-9000?
- Is the registrar local or will this be a long distance relationship? Don't dismiss a long distance relationship if the registrar seems right, but it does involve an extra cost. Try to find out what the costs are, including their application fees, initial visit costs, the

certification audit costs and expenses, cost of future surveillance audits, three-year reassessment policy, and cancellation fees.

- Is the potential registrar your type? Do they know about your type of business, and can they talk your language? Do you have the same interests, are they authorized to grant certification to your type of business, have they worked with other people in your line of business, can they give you a reference in your industry to call?

- Are they available? When you call, do they speak with you or pass you around? Do they meet the 48-hour return-your-call test? Can they meet with you for an introductory chat? Can they specify when they could perform the certification audit?

- Is the agency expensive? Don't be misled by an artificially low initial quote with the intention of accelerating the meter later. They are all fairly competitive; however, be leery of a casual "couple of people for a couple of days" quote. Respect the person who might want to go to a place where you can talk and enjoy yourselves; that's how good relationships are built.

- Now, for the most important question: Do you like each other? Do they approach you with a positive attitude—one that indicates they want to make it a positive experience for both of you, that they are really interested in your passing the audit? Do they realize that you may be a bit nervous and are they open and patient with your exploring questions? Do they respond quickly and accurately to your inquiries? Your questions may be similar to the following:

  — How often will you stop by and visit? Some certifiers visit every 6 months, others only once a year. There are advantages and disadvantages either way.

  — How long in advance will you call before you come? Some registrars lay out a three-year schedule and allow you to look and be your best when they get there. Others call only two weeks before they plan to arrive. While this can be very uncomfortable, especially if you have a busy schedule or a full house of customers, it is palatable, but rarely can you look and feel your best. Don't assume that you can only spruce up just before they get there—they know how to get an accurate reading regardless of your preparation.

- How do they view the world? Some registrars only see black or white, pass or fail, when they score you after the certification audit. Others see shades of passing or failing and give a range of scores. They will all ask the same kinds of questions and look in the same places, but some are better at looking than others and do have somewhat different interpretations of what they see versus what they believe the standard requires.

- How tough are they? What is their position on preassessment versus going for the certificate on the first try without the rehearsal? What if you don't pass on the first try of the certification audit? It usually depends on how badly you missed the points and where. Each registrar has a different approach. One may say "we will be back within 30 days" and then will only look at your shortfalls, provided they weren't major points (e.g., a Class I hit). At the other extreme, another may say "don't hold your breath," meaning that you're back to square one. Ask for, and be sure to negotiate, a follow-up date once you have set up the agreement for the first audit, just in case you don't make it the first time. QS-9000 is a fairly new and interpretive standard and therefore has gray areas. Try to find an accredited registrar who understands your business. Get to know the probable lead auditor and find out the interpretation of some of the questions that you might not be able to resolve. This will allow you to calibrate your initial approach to the lead auditor's expectations. In addition, make it clear to your agency that you want someone who knows your industry's practices and has common sense.

- Confirm that your registrar is financially sound and scout out how their auditors were trained and who they work for. Some registrars actually outsource the audits to independent agencies, and you have to ask yourself whether that is in your best interest. You also want to make sure the auditors have been trained to a standard such as ASQC's Certified Quality Auditor standard.

- If you should pass the certification audit, how will you be able to announce it to the world? You need to find out not only exactly how you can inform your customers, but also how they will be informing other registrars. In most cases, you are placed in an easily accessible registry where customers and competitors alike can look you up.

Step 5: Define Quality Responsibility

After the QS-9000 steering council has been educated, begin the process of clearly defining the responsibility for quality and the associated processes, from the president down through the entire organization. The definition of responsibility does not necessarily indicate that the individual has to be dedicated solely to quality full time; however, it does mean the organization has to demonstrate that an individual is actively involved in the quality management of a particular process and has that specific responsibility. This includes documented proof that there has been an activity associated with the defined responsibility. This may sound fairly easy and, surprisingly, it is. Start by laying out a matrix chart of the standard's elements against a rough flowchart of your organization with your steering council, and then have each of the QS-9000 team's members identify where their organization is affected by the standard as seen in Figure 4.1.

After they determine their areas of responsibility, have them sit with the other steering committee members for a review and nominate a primary owner of that element. This owner becomes the key coordinator for all activities associated with the element. You might discover that you're responsible for more than you think, or that some people think they have responsibilities that you think you have, or that no one has responsibility for certain areas. In any case, this can have ramifications beyond the scope of your council. If so, don't let this get in the way, but go to the top, explain your problem, ask for direction, and make it clear why it is so critical. Also ask for a decision date. This exercise accomplishes two tasks:

- It becomes the basis for your quality manual.
- It is a basic step in defining how your organization satisfies its customers and enables you to establish who is doing what.

To assist the auditors, you should create an organization chart that supports your definition of how the responsibility flows. This becomes the basis for your top-level quality manual and probably looks just like your current organization chart (just be sure the titles match your description of those responsible).

QS9000 Section I	QS Section Description	Production	Purchasing	Production Control	Mktg & Sales	Engineering	Logistics	MIS	Human Resources	Training	Quality Control	Quality Assurance
4.1	Management Responsibility	X	X	X	X	X	X	X	X	X	X	X
4.2	Quality System	X	X	X	X	X	X	X	X	X	X	X
4.3	Contract System	X	X	X	P	X	X	X				X
4.4	Design Control	X	X	X	X	P					X	X
4.5	Document and Data Control	X	X	X	X	P	X	X	X	X	X	X
4.6	Purchasing		P	X	X	X	X				X	X
4.7	Control of Customer Supplied Product	X		P	X	X	X	X			X	
4.8	Product Identification and Traceability	X	X	X	X	X	X	X			X	
4.9	Process Control	X	X	X	X	X	X	X	X	X	X	X
4.10	Inspection and Testing	X	X	X	X						P	X
4.11	Control of Inspection, Measuring, and Test Equipment	X	X	X		X	X				P	X
4.12	Inspection and Test Status	X			X						P	
4.13	Control of Nonconforming Product	X	X	X	X	X	X	X	X	X	X	X
4.14(a)	Corrective and	X	X	X	X	X	X	X	X	X	P	X
4.14(b)	Preventive Action	X	X	X	X	X	X	X	X	X	P	X

FIGURE 4.1.   QS-9000 responsibility matrix.

QS9000 Section I	QS Section Description	Production	Purchasing	Production Control	Mktg & Sales	Engineering	Logistics	MIS	Human Resources	Training	Quality Control	Quality Assurance
4.15	Handling, Storage, Packaging, Preservation, and Delivery	X	X	X	X	X	P				X	
4.16	Control of Quality Records	X	X	X		X		X	X	X	X	X
4.17	Internal Quality Awards										P	P
4.18	Training	X	X	X	X	X	X	X	X	P	X	X
4.19	Servicing	P		X	X	X	X	X		X	X	X
4.20	Statistical Techniques	X	X	X	X	X	X	X	X	X	X	X

FIGURE 4.1. (*continued*)

63

Step 6: Establish a Procedure Structure

Before you start writing procedures, your group should determine the format of the procedures as well as the best and most efficient method for maintaining this structure once it is established. This structure is the area that will require the greatest effort in preparation for the audit, and it will have a significant impact on your long-term procedure maintenance efficiency, so it deserves significant thought and effort.

One strategy is to develop four layers of procedures. Consider a pyramid approach, where a few, relatively stable procedures reside at the top, and the vast number of dynamic procedures (e.g., work instructions) and the specification and record type documents reside at the base. This approach minimizes the number of procedures and dramatically reduces the maintenance and coordination requirements. The QS-9000 standard formally describes the system as follows:

Level I:	Quality Manual
II:	Procedures that generally define an activity
III:	"Job" or "work" instructions that detail the activity
IV:	Miscellaneous documents and detailed specifications that provide details and records supporting a task.

In this layered structure, the top or corporate level is relatively general and primarily focused on the various standards that are being supported, how to approach QS-9000 requirements, and the definition of the corporate quality assurance responsibilities. It should be brief.

It is likely that your existing quality procedures will need to be restructured. At a minimum, you will need to reference these procedures to the specific elements and order of the QS-9000 standard.

There is no one correct method for writing the actual procedures. We recommend that you allow each organization to generate the procedures in a fashion they are most comfortable with. The steering committee should set a framework for the minimum content requirements, then let the groups decide what works best for them. The framework should require at least a date of issuance, revision number, location for use, a QS-9000 reference number, any applicable safety precautions,

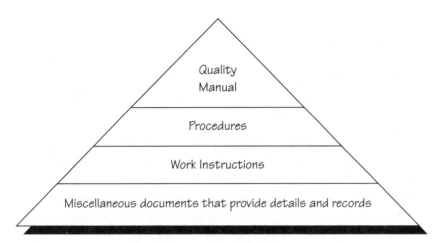

FIGURE 4.2.   A layered approach to procedures.

and a procedure name. Acceptable procedures that are already in place can be used, as long as it can be ensured that they meet the framework. Procedures can take many forms. Often, we see a storyboard format. In other instances, a flowchart may work the best. They can be in a database on a PC or in paper form. They can be on the backs of material transfer forms. They can be signs on the wall, visual acceptance criteria, or even copies of the operating instructions that came with the equipment with an added cover page for control. Let the groups be creative in how they solve their problem. The more hurdles you put in front of them, the slower their progress will be, so let them decide what they can use with the minimum of pain.

As procedures are being written, opportunities for standardization and replication in common areas shouldn't be missed. Establish a structure that can readily uncover these common areas before starting to avoid a lot of unnecessary duplication. One strategy is to define general procedures simply and then break out only the necessary details according to the organizations they represent. This way, procedures will be relatively general at the higher levels and get into detail only as required at the lower levels.

You must also establish measures for progress. The number of outstanding procedures to be written is one measure that you can suggest to the groups as an indicator of progress. Before you get started, you also need to define other requirements to ensure that the procedures incorporate all the critical QS-9000 requirements.

> **Tips—Quality Manuals:** The Tier 1 quality manual became the backbone for the QS-9000 effort as it defined who was responsible for what. In a very similar way, a Tier 2 manual was established by each organizational group to further define responsibilities in each of their groups. If their group was not involved, they simply left the Tier 1 detail in their manual. While this created some redundancy between their Tier 1 and Tier 2, this manual ensured that the group was involved and had not only further defined their roles but also demonstrated that they understand the roles of other groups.

Step 7: Define Documentation Standards

In this phase, the steering council must define and clarify all the documents required by the QS-9000 standard. They should also identify as many of the commonly used documents as possible to save work for the organization.

Divide the needed documents and procedures among the team members. Prototype these documents in a single area first, and once the process is debugged, get the council to endorse them. Consider starting with the Corrective Action Response (CAR) Process, possibly in all your operations and agree to this early on in the development. Have each member go to his or her area and do the installation. They may make their own adjustments, and that's all right as long as they stay within the framework and document it to satisfy the standard. Try to make one document serve as many purposes as possible.

The following is a listing of the documents that must be generated and the records that must exist to support the standard.

Documentation

- Quality Policy, Objectives, and Plans   (4.1.1)
- Quality Manual   (4.2)
- Design Control/APQP/PPAP   (4.4)
- Engineering Change Control   (4.5)

- Work Instructions/Procedures   (4.9.1)
- Final Inspections   (4.10.3)
- Instrument Calibration   (4.11.c)
- Nonconformities   (4.13)
- Corrective Actions and Customer Complaints (4.14)
- Handling, Storage, Packing, Delivery   (4.15)
- Internal Quality Audits   (4.17)

System Records

- Management Review   (4.1.3)
- Subcontractors Assessment   (4.6.2)
- Preventive Maintenance   (4.9)
- Instrument Calibration & Maintenance   (4.11.f)
- Audit Records   (4.17)
- Training   (4.18)

Contract/Product Records

- Contract Review   (4.3)
- Design Verification   (4.4.5.a)
- Product Identification   (4.8)
- Inspection, Testing   (4.10.4)
- Delivery Records   (4.15.6)
- Product Release   (4.12)
- Nonconforming Products   (4.13.1)

The standard must be interpreted according to how you conduct your operations. For example, a company that sells standard catalog items will maintain a different set of contract records than one that builds a custom part for a chassis. Assembly documentation doesn't have to be a drawing, it can be a photo or a prototype with a part number written on it. The only requirement is that you control these drawings, photos, or models to ensure that the proper item is being built at the right time and being tested according to the control plan.

There is an unlimited number of ways you can satisfy the requirements for documentation. The following sections provide additional insight into two of your primary documents: the quality manual and training records.

Quality Manual.

The quality manual reflects the essence of how you plan to run the business. You should make this manual as user friendly as possible. You want your employees to actually use it, and it is likely that your customers will request copies as well. The easiest approach would be to construct your manuals in your own words following the QS-9000 format—that is, with the same section order and the same contents being addressed as the standard. Consider a multilevel approach to your manual as described for procedures. And remember that the more you write, the more there is to audit—be brief.

Training Records.

We all live with the fear that some untrained rookie will come and repair our car's brakes, the plane's landing gear, or the control system of a nuclear power plant. The people who put our products together and take our orders need training and their functions must be strategic. QS-9000 requires that training takes place, that it is reasonable for the given task, and that its effectiveness is audited. The auditors look for the training records that are maintained for every important task affecting the product. For example, records must show that employees know how to operate the equipment associated with their jobs, that they have been trained on the assembly process, and in all cases, how they differentiate between good and bad workmanship. As you go through your procedure development, you will identify those tasks that affect the product, and from there you will be able to systematically identify the education and training needed for the job. These records can then become the basis for a job description (which is also required).

Before completing the training records, supervisors should sit down with a group of employees performing the job and together identify what is required to perform the task. They should then create a checklist of the key tasks or job functions for which training should be given followed by a confirmation of the employees' capabilities. At the end of this exercise, each employee performing a task will have a training record with the supervisor signed-off on the employee's ability to perform the task prior to his or her being left alone on the job.

It is likely that you do not have a training record for everyone who is performing a job for which it is required. In this case, a retroactive training record is acceptable, as long as you specify this is a one-time start-up policy. When Span was audited, it was noted that there was quite a bit of "wet ink" on the documents. That was acceptable because the activities complied with the current procedures and the appropriate records were in place and demonstrated a "reasonable period of compliance." What is a reasonable period? If you can't decide, ask your auditor, as each situation is different.

Occasionally a job will be defined as requiring a degree. You may have people in such jobs that do not have a degree. Make sure you have a procedure in place to allow capable nongraduates to comply with your requirements. Define a process for waiving the requirement and show the evaluation methods with a checklist.

Finally, the training records should be readily accessible to the supervisors who are responsible for the records' accuracy and utilization. It is usually prudent to keep training records in the work areas, possibly having the employees maintaining their own set. Some operations have determined that the records are to be maintained in the personnel files. If this is the case, consider maintaining two personnel files, as a number of employees consider it an invasion of privacy when an auditor or outsider goes through their personal information while looking for training records.

If you let your employees maintain their own training records, they will take an interest in them and will generally ensure they are accurate. The better employees will also seek additional training and want to keep growing—this is a win-win situation. A sample training record form is illustrated in Figure 4.3.

> **Tip—Measurements:** The standard requires that you measure your operations not only for conformance but also for continuous improvement opportunities and customer satisfaction levels.
>
> Conformance measurement was achieved through some of the following methods:
>
> **Span Defect Management System (SDMS):** The SDMS process was simply a series of linked spreadsheets that collected base performance data at each work area. The data was loaded into a preordained format that would eventually roll up to senior management for the daily production meetings and monthly status reports. When a process moved out of control,

PERSONNEL TRAINING RECORD			
Name	Dept. #		
Title			
Education			
Formal Training			
Work Experience/On-the-Job Training			
Employee's Signature			
Supervisor's Signature			
Date			

FIGURE 4.3.   Sample training record form.

it was investigated, and appropriate corrective actions were taken. This state of control was based upon upper and lower specifications for performance. Not only do we respond when something goes wrong, we investigate to see what might have gone right and see if we can replicate the event. The data measured included rejects, output, reworks, and customer returns as well as hours, absentees, and the like. These defects and out-of-control states became the basis for continuous improvement projects.

Precontrol Charts: We made use of the Dorian Shannin method for ensuring that a process maintained a process capability of 1.6 or greater. In some of our long-run operations, we were able to conduct a full statistical study and establish Xbar and Range analysis charts. However they were somewhat difficult for our operators to use and required technical support. Dorian Shannin had developed a "banding" measurement method that allowed the operator to establish process control charts and ensure conformance. The methods are very simple: Begin by dividing the specification width by four. The quarters above and below the center line become a green zone. The quarters on each end of the specification width become a yellow zone. The areas outside of the specification become the red zones. The operator follows these rules and marks the results on the control chart.

This process is not only easy to use, it only requires an operator with a calculator, and they can make the appropriate notes that will allow for a corrective action. The specifications can also be easily tightened to accommodate a customer request.

Out of Box Audits (OBAs): A sampling system was put in place to determine what the customers see when they open their shipment. Just prior to shipment (after it has gone through our entire operation, including inspections), an inspector will randomly select and quarantine the entire shipment. They will proceed to tear it down to ensure its correctness. We look at approximately 4 percent of all the shipments and confirm not only that the product's performance meets specifications but also that all the administrative aspects of the shipment are met. This sampling system becomes part of our immediate feedback corrective action process as well as a projection of overall customer satisfaction.

Customer Satisfaction: We were able to come up with some fairly inexpensive and responsive measures that would provide a basic level of customer satisfaction estimation. The most obvious for

Span was the quality and on-time delivery reports that our larger customers were sending us. This told us how we were doing on their most critical measures. We supplemented our own on-time metrics with the OBAs to estimate the direction of customer acceptance.

Total Business Quality (TBQ) Metrics: The following is a sample of monthly report measures that indicate the overall health of the business with regard to the quality goal and QS-9000:

- Market Growth
  - Market Share
  - Win/Lose Ratios
  - Partnerships: Customer
  - Customer Satisfaction Index
- Speed And Service
  - Delivery Cycle
  - C-CARs (Customer-Corrective Action Requests)
  - Product Lead Times
  - Cycle Time For Repairs
- Quality
  - Warranty Cost
  - Returns
  - Out Of Box Audits
  - QCARs (Quality (internal) Corrective Action Requests)
  - Supplier Quality
  - In-Process Rejects By Area
- Productivity
  - Sales Per Employee
  - Waste/Inventory Turns
  - Scrap/Rework
  - MRB (Material Review Board/Bin)
  - Partnership Suppliers
  - Recycling
  - Credits (Product)
  - Cost Reductions
  - Continuous Improvement Efforts: Teams/$

Supplier Development: The standard requires that you work with your suppliers to ultimately improve the products that your customers receive from you. It requires that you have a system

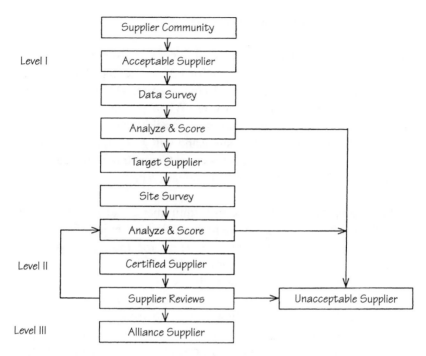

FIGURE 4.4.   Span instruments supplier alliance process.

in place to select a good supplier and to work with them to improve their capability. Again in a fast track effort, we brought together the purchasing manager, lead buyer, QA manager and
vice-president of quality to build a system that would not only
meet the intention of QS-9000, but also bring our costs down
and improve our quality. Over a 2-week period, we benchmarked
other similar company processes and came up with our own
Span Supplier Alliance Process (see Figure 4.4). We broke the
purchasing personnel up into commodity teams and began using the process that we had developed.

The auditors will not only be looking to see that you have
some process for supplier improvement and QS-9000 compliance, but will also ask you to cite an example or two of where
you have been working with them to improve the quality process.
You are most likely doing this in some form, but your team will
have to have a few examples ready for presentation.

Step 8: Educate All Employees on QS-9000

It takes a long time and repeated communications to get any message out to all corners of your organization. It is essential that everyone comprehend the meaning and requirements of QS-9000, as it requires the full participation of all employees. When you let everyone know why you are introducing an experience possibly perceived as painful, it will reduce the resistance to change and will gain support for continued compliance. An employee newsletter demonstrating the clear support of the senior member of the organization can be used to educate employees.

When employees understand the requirements and why it is important to the company, they are more likely to do a better job. Through education, employees are mentally prepared for the very exhaustive preparation and audit. This preparation leads to confidence, which is apparent when they meet with the auditors.

Ongoing education also includes training employees on dealing with the auditors and responding to their questions. The education process extends over several months and requires multiple levels of communications before the general population understands what QS-9000 is all about. During this phase, continue to communicate the company's quality policy, as this will be part of the auditor's inquiry. You might also consider posting your quality policy every 60 feet or on the backs of ID badges and be confident that sooner or later the message will get through.

Keeping the management abreast of the organization's progress will also help the cause. By posting your progress measures, broken down by organization, you will ensure that those falling behind will receive the appropriate peer pressure (no senior managers want their organization to be the reason for the company not being ready). About a month before the audit, you might want supervisors to hold group meetings across the company for final preparation and to answer final questions.

Step 9: Develop Operational QS-9000 Management Teams

After educating the QS-9000 steering council and preparing the documents and procedures, it becomes necessary to introduce this information to the organization and build momentum to execute the various elements of the program. Members of the QS-9000 steering council can accomplish this by setting up operational units within their own organizations, usually by department, educating them, and then going about installing the QS-9000 elements that are relevant to that group.

The QS-9000 management teams should consist of senior members of the various organizations with key supervision from each one of their groups. Their primary tasks should encompass at least the following:

- Defining the flow within their organizations that will determine the areas affected by QS-9000 (using flowcharts). Reconcile duties at intersection points.
- Possibly building their own Tier 2 manual.
- Administer the progress measures.
- Assume responsibility for their areas' conformance.

The QS-9000 management team members, once educated, act as the resident experts. When questions come up that they are unable to address, or do not feel comfortable with, the issues are brought to the QS-9000 steering council. The QS-9000 steering council develops a position or contacts the lead auditor of the certification agency for a disposition. The compliance process should be managed on a weekly basis with the appropriate indicators in place to ensure visibility.

This is when the project really gets its wings and develops a personality of its own. Encourage people to get involved and use the management-by-walking-around technique. There will be those who aggressively ask questions; answer them quickly. But don't assume that because some people aren't asking questions, all is well. In the beginning, they are most likely assimilating the changes and new requirements.

Step 10: Perform Procedure Upgrades

Procedure upgrades will probably occur at all levels of the organization, and in some cases this can involve an enormous amount of work. For most companies these procedures typically belong to the quality or industrial engineering departments, neither of which is staffed to support the load required to bring procedures up to compliance. While you may have procedures in place, in some areas they may be written in a way that is entirely different from the way the job is performed—this is quite common.

If you have effectively deployed your operational QS-9000 teams, they have identified the major informational flows and understand the documentation and record requirements. They have been able to identify where procedures are required. It's at this point that you should bring the real power of QS-9000 to bear—your employees. Employees know the actual task better than anyone else in your organization. Consider having them create the procedures. If you allow them to do this, you will enjoy the following pleasant benefits as we did at Span:

- A potentially enormous work load is spread over a large group of employees rather than a few. This ensures a shorter duration of the activity.
- The most qualified and most knowledgeable individuals write the procedures ensuring that the practices align with the document.
- The employees become part of the process and feel like part of a team that is striving for the same common goal. You might even hear statements like "the company is finally starting to listen to us!"

Some in your organization may question the ability of their employees to write procedures, and in some areas they might be correct, but with a little help from their supervisors, most employees can draft a box and diamond flowchart. You can even write it up into a storyboard format later, but that isn't necessary.

Once you have the draft procedure ready, have it reviewed by all the employees who perform the task. You might discover some disagreement. Treat this as an opportunity for a small group to go out and figure out the best of all worlds. We have a documented case where the yields in one of our areas showed a dramatic increase because of this exercise. Once the mini-team has come up with the best method, have all the employees sign the procedures. Not only will you have a training record that demonstrates the employee has been trained, you will also have a record of who else can perform the job in an employee's absence. You will also notice a higher sense of ownership among the em-

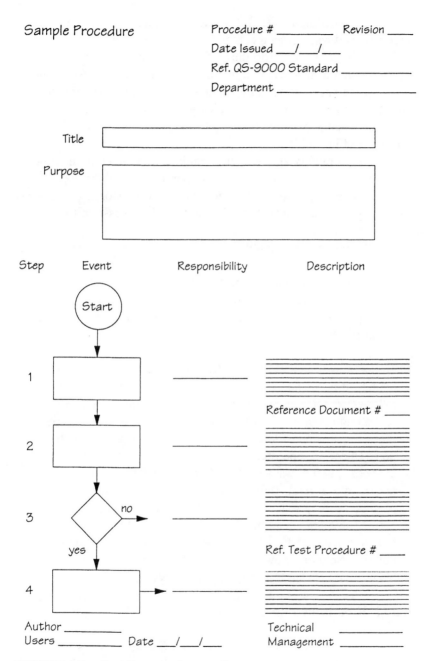

FIGURE 4.5.   Sample procedure outline.

ployees and a willingness to follow the procedures. Should they have a suggestion and want a change, they know where to go.

Any changes to the procedures should require a full review by all employees and a new set of signatures. This is effective for ensuring that everyone participates in the change and prevents the "no one ever told me" response. Also you will quickly reveal any objections or problems to the change prior to installing the upgrade and driving the group into a state of instability.

Keep your quality and industrial engineers involved in the process to ensure that the tasks and tools are proper and that all the appropriate safety practices are invoked. Procedures should be stored in the areas where they are used and where they are easily accessible to the employees performing the task.

Finally, procedures should be the property of the local supervision and management. It needs to be made clear that maintaining structural process integrity is as much a part of the job as building the product. The direct management should be responsible for controlling how their operation performs as well as their operation's ability to meet compliance requirements.

Tip—Procedures and Work Instructions: Generally a procedure defines a particular workflow or set of activities that must be followed to correctly perform a task. A procedure could be detailed enough to allow for the execution of a task. Should operators require more detail, you might consider a work instruction. Once an operator has been successfully trained the chances that they will ever go back and revisit these documents are remote at best. Don't spend a lot of money making these perfect as they will most likely change before you complete them. The more visual the better. Where possible, try to use a box and diamond flowchart to define you process. Substitute Polaroid pictures or even a sample of the finished item for verbiage. Just be sure to keep them under control.

Step 11: Establish Corrective Action Tracking

One of the required elements of QS-9000, Section 4.14, is the establishment of a corrective action process. It calls for the establishment of a structured process that addresses methods used to prevent the reoc-currence of a problem and to employ an audit process that continually ensures that your operations meet the standard. This is one of the most effective tools you can employ in the transition of your organization.

Historically, when an audit team sweeps through the areas to verify compliance to the defined system, they may find a nonconformity. A nonconformity would prompt the creation of a document noting the fail-ure with the expectation that it would be resolved within a reasonable time frame. A problem occurs when the organization only addresses the individual item identified by the audit team. For example, in the past, if an audit uncovered an untrained employee, the response from the group would have been simply to go back and train that employee. The pre-ferred response would be to determine the root cause for the employee not being trained and to fix the process that allowed this to occur.

To remedy this undesirable type of response and promote process improvement, we developed a document called a Quality Corrective Action Request (QCAR) as seen in Figure 4.6.

The QCAR looks for the correction of the root cause of the prob-lem, not the symptom. It requires identification of a plan with a time-table for implementation and agreement between the initiator (auditor) and the operation that the root cause of the nonconformance will be corrected. Tracking the QCAR status by your audit teams provides the second key measure for the readiness of your organization—how much needs to be fixed. A drawback to the QCAR approach is that it usually takes longer to make the symptom go away. But the disease is cured and the patient thrives.

Tip—Corrective and Preventive Action Requests: The QS-9000 standard requires a corrective and preventive action process. The team determined that a single process and form could be used to address all kinds of corrective and preventive actions from a number of sources. A single Quality Corrective Action Response (QCAR) process was initiated and tracked from a single point.

The QCAR was used extensively by the audit teams along with: quality assurance when a preventive action was observed, by the sales organization when a consistent nonconformance was observed, and even interdepartmentally when an upstream

Span Instruments Quality Corrective Action Request				
#1	QCAR #: DATE:	☐ INT ☐ EXT	CORRECTIVE ☐	PREVENTATIVE ☐

#2	TO:	RETURN TO: **SPAN INSTRUMENTS** ORIGINATOR'S NAME: ADDRESS:
	DEPARTMENT:	

#3	CLASSIFICATION OF DEFECT	NONCONFORMANCE REPORT #:
	☐ CRITICAL ☐ MAJOR ☐ MINOR	ORDER #:
	REQUIRED RESPONSE (WORKING DAYS)	REF DOC:
	_____DAYS ☐ 15 DAYS ☐ 30 DAYS	LOT QTY: REJECTED QTY:
	☐ IMPLEMENT NEXT ORDER	SUPPLIER PART #:
	PART NUMBER:	

#4	PART DESCRIPTION:
#5	DESCRIPTION OF DISCREPANCY (INCLUDE DATA)

THE FOLLOWING TO BE FILLED OUT BY THE PERSON ASSIGNED TO THE PROBLEM.

#6	VERIFIED ROOT CAUSE:
#7	ACTION PLAN (CORRECTIVE OR PREVENTITIVE):
#8	CONTROLS TO PREVENT RECURRENCE / OCCURANCE. (ATTACH DATA/RESULTS DEMONSTRATING IMPROVEMENT.) :

#9	COMPLETION DATE:	DATE IMPLEMENTED:
#10	SIGNATURE:	DEPT: DATE:

THE FOLLOWING TO BE FILLED OUT BY THE ORIGINATOR

#11	ORIGINATOR TO VERIFY AND APPROVE: APPROVAL ☐ YES ☐ NO VERIFIED BY: DATE:
#12	REASON FOR NON APPROVAL:

FORM 01-011.DOC (A)   09/05/96

FIGURE 4.6.   Span QCAR form.

Quality Corrective Action Request
- Procedure For Completing This Form -

Section #	**Originator fills in sections 1 through 5**

#1 Fill in date issued. QCAR number will be assigned by quality control.
Check off internal for QCAR's used within span.
Check off external for QCAR's sent to suppliers.
Check off corrective for QCAR's initiated for problem found.
Check off preventative for QCAR's initiated to prevent problems from occurring in the future

#2 Fill in where the QCAR is to go. If external, supplier's name, address, person's name. If internal, fill in name, department. Fill in where the QCAR is to be returned to; originator's name and department. Address to be filled in only if sent to outside supplier.

#3 Check off classification of defect and the required response time. If applicable, reference any ncmr numbers. Indicate purchase order # if external, or, if internal, reference the number that describes this order or job. Indicate the part# and/or model # of the defective part. Fill in the lot quantity. Fill in the quantity of rejected parts found during the sample inspection or test. Fill in the supplier's part #.

#4 Brief description of the part.

#5 Describe the defect or problem, giving all known facts such as what is the nonconforming specification and any other data that would help the person in completing 7 through 11.

The document is then given to the quality control documentation specialist to log into the database and assign a QCAR number. After the QCAR number has been assigned the QCAR will be routed to the person assigned to do the corrective action. If an outside vendor the QCAR will be routed to the purchasing manager and he in turn will pass QCAR on to outside vendor.

Sections 6 through 10 to be filled out by the person assigned to the problem.

#6 Indicate the root causes: who, what, when and why.

#7 Indicate the corrective action plan: who, what, when.

#8 Indicate what controls have been put in place to prevent the problem from recurring. Attach data / results that demonstrate improvement.

#9 Indicate the completion date of the corrective action and when implemented.

#10 Person responsible for filling out section 7 through 11 must sign and fill in department. Fill in the date the report is signed.

Send the QCAR back to the originator or purchasing manager if an outside vendor.

Originator fills in sections 11 and 12

#11 If corrective action is approved then check off the yes box and sign and date and, attach data that validated the approval. Return QCAR to quality control documentation specialist.

#12 If approval is not given, check off the no box and indicate reason. Send the QCAR back to the person responsible for corrective action.

FORM 01-011.DOC (A)   09/05/96

FIGURE 4.6. *(continued).*

practice affected the performance of a downstream group. The key was to determine the root cause and have the source of the nonconformance address it with effective action within a defined time frame.

Step 12: Train Internal Audit Teams

Self-audits provide you with insight into the status of your operations and are required for compliance to QS-9000. The faster you can deploy the teams, the faster you can begin to fix things. It is fairly common for a group of external or corporate auditors to come by once a year and take a sample survey of the level of your organization's compliance and provide you with some form of a findings list. This is a good approach for determining major problem areas, but it does not necessarily provide the organization with the refined visibility needed to successfully survive a QS-9000 audit. Have the external auditors perform what is considered a systems audit. Systems audits review the standard and ensure that all the items are addressed in each group and that all the interconnects between the groups are defined. Consider establishing an auditing group composed of individuals familiar with the organization and have them perform procedural audits, stepping through the details of the procedures and work instructions and comparing them with the actual practices of those performing the tasks.

For example, suppose you come across a mouse in your kitchen. You call in the exterminator, a couple of traps are placed, and the next day a single mouse is caught. Did the exterminator confirm that you had a mouse? Yes. Were all the mice caught? Probably not. Remember the saying, "If you see one mouse, you have a dozen." There is a high probability that you will discover another mouse. Bringing in an exterminator on a one-shot basis just doesn't work. It is better to have a cat that is relatively inexpensive to maintain in return for its vigilance and hunting expertise. An external or formal corporate team goes around annually and gives you a picture of the types of problems you might have. In addition, create a group of cats—that is, procedural internal audit teams.

The primary purpose of the procedural audit team is to promote the self-auditing of an organization and to provide the visibility that a systems or external auditor lacks. We started with the premise that the employees who were involved in the work were most likely to know what was really happening in their own organizations and were therefore the ideal candidates to be on the internal procedural audit teams. We selected members from different parts of the organization and trained them on the requirements of QS-9000 and on how to conduct an audit. In a larger organization you might consider a pilot in one plant first. Then send the remaining operations through the training. One trained auditor can develop a course that will produce some very effective auditors.

In a typical plant, the procedural audit team could consist of a buyer, a planner, an assembler, a warehouse person, and an internal certified lead auditor who meets ASQC guidelines to form a complete plant mini-audit team. In the case of Span, this team developed an aggressive schedule and went about auditing the organization. However, before the teams were sent out to do audits and generate QCARs, we recognized that we would need to change the mind-set of our management. Our management had developed an adverse reception to audits and especially to findings. Yet we needed management to look at the findings, QCARs, in a positive manner.

We first convinced our senior managers that a QCAR issuance was in fact a positive event, and fortunately they had a positive response. They realized that as they were pushing their organization to move ahead quickly with scarce resources, some things would fall through the cracks. It's similar to a good basketball player—the better ones get four fouls in a game because they are playing aggressively while the ones who don't get any fouls either aren't being aggressive or they are on the bench. The senior managers took this position and reinforced it with their management teams.

This approach with the audit teams had some very positive effects on the organization:

- Self-audit reduces the amount of anxiety within the operation. It had management support and was viewed as a method for improvement by supervisors and employees.
- Having the existing staff perform the audits on a part-time basis reduced the need to fund additional staff.
- Employees look upon this training as an opportunity for growth as well as a return of control over their environment.

- Procedural audit teams are able to review the operations with their peers in a nonthreatening manner, yielding a higher level of cooperation.
- The same audit team can also support a supplier survey program, applying QS-9000 standards to suppliers. This also answered a common claim by suppliers that we might be holding them to a higher standard than our own organization. Employees are also likely to enjoy the opportunity to travel to a supplier's site, as it can generate some great ideas.
- Self-audit teams become ambassadors and interpreters during the certification audit. When the QS-9000 auditors descend on your operations, they will speak "QS-ese" and probably won't understand your company terminology, nor do they understand your operations and systems. Each company "speaks" with a lot of homegrown terms and acronyms, and the members of the mini-audit teams can be excellent translators. This is critical for ensuring that the proper messages are being communicated and reducing the stress between the groups, auditors, and the company. Your own auditors can also help your employees feel more comfortable when approached by an auditor and can sometimes translate the questions into words the employee can understand. The company audit team members should ensure that the QS-9000 auditors are being guided to the correct locations and that the responses fit the questions. If an auditor receives an answer that seems incorrect, the issue can be dealt with before it escalates to a finding or observation. The self-audit team member can also ensure that the auditors are receiving their answers quickly, as there is nothing more frustrating to an auditor than waiting for answers. During the audit at Span, there were always two audit assist members from our audit teams with each QS-9000 auditor. It was common for a QS-9000 auditor to ask a question that would require one of the audit assist members to chase someone or something down, while the other remained behind to answer questions or escort the auditor. Most companies require visitors to be escorted, and this includes auditors. You have an obligation for their safety and to ensure that they are always taken to the correct locations.

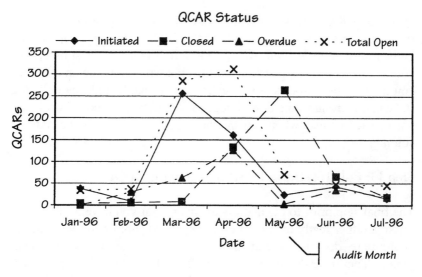

FIGURE 4.7.   Status of QCARs leading up to Span instrument's audit.

As stated earlier, your audit teams can provide tremendous visibility in assessing your readiness as well as projecting when you will be able to sustain a successful audit. At Span, we tracked the number of QCARs generated by the audit teams in the areas that indicated they were prepared for an audit. We considered the issuance of a QCAR as a positive indicator, and the retirement of a QCAR as another positive measure. We looked at open QCARs, those that had not yet been fixed, as less desirable, but also recognized that fixing a root cause of a problem often took time. Therefore, outstanding QCARs were considered more as an outstanding workload to be completed than as a problem. There was no pressure unless the organization had missed its own committed completion date. These measures were reported even to the president, who of course cheered on the management to generate QCARs.

More than 425 QCARs were initiated in the areas that claimed they were prepared for the audit. The status of the QCARs leading up to the audit are illustrated in Figure 4.7.

The QS-9000 audit at Span occurred in May of 1996, 5½ months after we had set out to achieve QS-9000, and we still had not closed all of our QCARs. However, we did make sure they were minor and their fix status was well documented. The QS-9000 auditors, not surprisingly, found more on their own. The moral of this story is simple; start your audits as soon as possible with people who know the areas! Once you have some initial data suggesting a reasonable audit date, "put a stake in the ground" and don't budge! You will be amazed at how much you can accomplish when you and the organization can see the auditors coming.

Step 13: Pull Together a PPAP Based on the APQP

The final step prior to the audit is to ensure that you have a PPAP submission either ready to submit or an approved submission with all the appropriate documents and signatures from your automotive customers. The PPAP draws very heavily from the APQP. The APQP must be pulled together with all the defined documents referenced and structured such that the auditor can look at the PPAP and find all the supporting information in the APQP.

> **Tip—Design Control:** A small team (the vice-presidents of engineering and quality) got together over a weekend and redesigned the entire product development process to meet the flow and requirements of the APQP. We also benchmarked a couple of other similar company product development efforts and ended up with a hybrid that would yield not only compliance, but more important a strategy for a focused and optimal rapid product introduction process. We needed to ensure that not only would the product work as promised for a targeted MTBF (Mean Time Between Failure) but just as important, it would yield a maximum life-cycle cost reduction opportunity. In a number of studies, it has been identified that up to 85 percent of a product's full life-cycle cost is committed as soon as the initial product drawings are complete. The follow-on operations (such as purchasing and production) can only affect the remaining 15 percent. The difference between companies that achieve a 15 percent profit before tax versus a 24 percent can usually point to a lower-cost design and ideal integration into the capability of the manufacturing operations. The financial im-

pact is usually not felt for a couple of years into the manufacturing of the product as the products begin to meet their full potential in sales volume and warranty cost.

Step 14: Certification Audit

Now the fun begins. Your sales force has probably already promised
the world that you will have certification and will most likely blame
you for every order they lose until you become certified. The financial
people have planned all those promised cost savings into next year's
budget, and now your president's career is tied in. You have continually
reminded everyone that they don't want to be the ones that cause the
company to fail—and you realize that goes for you too!

Where can it go wrong? According to the largest registrar, the root
cause for findings are usually based on the following:

- Lack of understanding of the standard.
- Lack of management commitment.
- Lack of resources.
- Customs of the trades.

The certifying audit is extremely rigorous and comprehensive.
Every site that was visited at Span confirmed that "they don't miss anything, but they are fair."

Figure 4.8 is a schedule illustrating the minimum number of labor
days that the auditors will be at your location for both the first certification visit and six month follow-up. In addition, they will be visiting all
your shifts of operation. Sometimes it will seem excessive, but the auditors must abide by these guidelines.

A dedicated office area should be set aside for the auditors' use during their stay, and it should include copies of all the relevant documents
they will require to get started. Your corporate manual and each operation's top-level manual should be kept there as well.

Treat the auditors as welcome guests, not as hostile, adversarial
forces. Put yourself in their place—they are often away from home facing the discomforts of business travel like hotels, airports, long car
rides, late planes, and rarely a good sound sleep. Usually their interac-
tions with people on the job are somewhat strained, given the nature of

Certificated Entity: Number of Employees	Initial Audit (On-Site Labor Days)	Ongoing Six-Month Surveillance Audits: (On-Site Labor Days)
1–15	2	1
16–30	4	1
31–60	5	1.5
61–100	6	1.5
101–250	8	2
251–500	10	2.5
501–1000	12	3
1001–2000	15	3.5
2001–4000	18	4.5
4001–8000	21	5.5

FIGURE 4.8.　Survey audit day requirements.

their work, and when the job is done, they have a mountain of paperwork to do. See that they get good rooms on the quiet side of the hotel. If there is a suite, consider the expense as an investment in having a more rested auditor visiting your site. A little consideration in these areas is appreciated, especially if you are attempting to demonstrate and prove a critical position with an exhausted auditor. Attention to these details supports your self-portrayal as a company focused on quality at all times and levels.

Prior to the auditor's arrival, ensure that all the QS-9000 steering council members know their roles and are ready to act as escorts between areas, along with your mini-auditors, if appropriate. The steering council should consider meeting daily during the audit to review the previous day's results and implement plans to correct any findings prior to the conclusion of the audit. Depending on the type of agency you are using, it may be possible to correct a minor finding prior to the registrar leaving the premises, which could help you meet the minimum requirement or reduce the follow-up audit duration.

Once the auditors are on site, bring them to your conference room and begin the orientation to the manuals as well as to the various safety and escort requirements. As stated earlier, promote a very open and friendly atmosphere. The auditors should have been selected with the understanding that they want you to succeed. On the other hand, they have their reputation to protect, and the possibility of losing their certification is very real. Their job is to ensure that you have:

- Established a quality policy.
- Developed an appropriate quality system.
- Documented the system as required.
- Effectively implemented the system.
- Met the requirements of the QS-9000 standard.

A typical audit proceeds in the following manner. You greet the auditors, conduct the orientation, and assign team members. The lead auditor then takes control of the audit, and from then on the approach is at the discretion of this individual. One of the first stops might be a visit to your formal internal audit group where the auditors will ask to see the last year's internal audits. They want to confirm that you are actually conducting audits and will want to see schedules and activities associated with the audits, such as follow-ups to previous findings. They are also looking for trends, where your own audit teams repeatedly find problems. They will take their cues from the findings of these audits and look in the same areas. Finally, they are looking for open findings that are critical to the standard. If your own audit organization has left an open critical finding, it is an immediate "gotcha." If it is critical, the auditors could simply go to the area identified, confirm the shortfall, and thank you for inviting them as they head home. It is absolutely critical that all open Class 1 findings are closed. A Class 1 finding is when you have failed to document a requirement of the standard or are failing to perform the requirement. A Class 2 finding is when you have it poorly documented or poorly conform to the documented requirements. When you do both poorly, it is up to the auditor whether it is a Class 1 or 2! You cannot become certified until all the Class 1 findings are cleaned up!

After the auditors are firmly convinced that you have an aggressive audit program, they might make one more stop, prior to moving ahead with the audit in earnest. This next stop provided us with visible proof of the thoroughness of their audit and should also help you realize, as one of our employees so aptly stated, "you can't hide anything." They might visit your local accounting organization to gain access to all your departmental account codes, thereby ensuring access to all the desired areas and organizations. If you were thinking about making an organization disappear or a tool room vanish, think again. Their methodology involved going to central information points first, looking for abnormalities, and then making sure their audit plan incorporated an investigation of these abnormalities.

A typical example was that of Span's calibration control. The audit team asked to see how calibration and the maintenance records were controlled. While they were verifying that the system existed, they also reviewed the records to see who had not returned tools and ensured we had conducted a measurement system analysis (MSA). These locations then became the primary focus for investigation. With the team now armed with account codes and a complete pass of internal audit data they begin the process of investigation. This process usually follows the flow of the product, which in the case of QS-9000, means all the way back to your sales office and verification of your marketing literature to your PPAP submission, backed up by your APQP.

You can expect that they will visit a local sales branch (if it is in your factory, that will be the logical target). They will ask where the orders come in, pick one up, and then say, "Show me." The show-me involves asking the employees how they handle orders, how orders are entered, and what do they do when they have a problem. The auditors may ask you to show them some training records (for both inside and outside employees, even the sales people if appropriate) and possibly ask questions like, "Do you have a quality policy? What is it?"

After the employees have overcome their initial nervousness, they point to the wall (where your quality policy is posted) and say, "That's it," point to the back of their badges where the quality policy has been placed or simply mumble something about excellence and they begin answering the questions and showing the necessary documents. When the auditors are satisfied, they will migrate down through your order scheduling department to again ask similar questions, with the focus on verifying that you are accurately processing the order, quoting deliveries, and handling the exceptions.

Finally, your order makes it to the production areas, and there the audit team might split up. The majority of the auditor's time, as much as 80 percent, will be spent in the manufacturing process. The rest of the audit team migrates up through engineering, design, and marketing.

As the audit team goes through engineering and design, the primary focus will be on two areas. A potential trouble spot can be the coordination of documentation between manufacturing and engineering. They will want to see not only that the proper documents are sent to manufacturing, but also that some form of acknowledgment is sent back to the originator ensuring that manufacturing has actually seen the documents. The other area is in the APQP and PPAP. The auditors will be looking for a process that ensures the product meets both the performance and safety requirements that it claims to support. They will also want to see your PPAP submission. They will want to see a signature that verifies that what has been designed is what marketing asked for and what is being communicated to manufacturing.

The audit team will eventually migrate up to the marketing organization and verify the communication process between engineering and marketing. They will also look to ensure that what marketing is selling is in fact what engineering is being asked to design.

Meanwhile, the audit team on the assembly floor is interacting with your plant people. They will spend most of their time on the manufacturing floor and will generally avoid the supervision. They will walk into an area, introduce themselves, and ask what the employee does. After the employee describes his or her tasks to the auditor and it is relevant to the auditor's area of inquiry, the employee can expect additional questions such as:

- Do you have a quality policy here?
- Tell me about this machine, how do you operate it?
- Where are the procedures you consult if you have any questions? (The employees must be able to have easy access and personally show the auditor.)
- Were you trained before you started working alone, and could you get that record for me?
- How do you know when you are making the product correctly? Can you tell when it is good or bad? Show me. (Make sure there is some documented method for differentiation and that it was included as part of the training record.)
- If you have a problem with the machine or material coming out, what do you do? (You will need a documented process outlined on how you control nonconforming materials.)

- How do you know those tools you are using are acceptable? Which ones need to be calibrated, and how do you know when to send them back?
- I noticed that you are using control charts. What do you do when they go out of control—like right there on the chart—what happened and what did you do? Could you show me the procedure and your training record on how you were trained on these charts? (Make sure your employees who are marking the charts are keeping records on those out-of-control events; the auditors are looking for some form of documented proof that the employee did take some action versus ignoring the event. Also ensure your charts are maintained on line in a dynamic fashion. Charts updated after the product has left the area are in jeopardy of being considered ineffective to your preventive program.)
- How do you know you are building the right thing? Could you show me the assembly documents or model?

After the auditor has completed his questions he will apply a score or make a binary decision based on the approach, the documentation, and the execution. The auditors will also look for documentation, old and current. Ensure that you have all your old documents (or models) removed or clearly marked, for example, "not for manufacturing use." They will be calling their fellow auditors who are visiting engineering and confirming revisions and dates. They will be looking at your test equipment to ensure not only that the equipment is under some form of calibration control, but also that the test requirements and outputs are those specified by engineering. They will look to see that your manufacturing operations have procedures for the update of these documents.

The auditors will progress through the operation to final testing, then to packaging, and on to shipping. They will also go into your service operations and will treat them as they would any manufacturing operation.

After finishing in the marketing and engineering areas, they will then descend on your materials organization. They will review your planning operations—make sure you have a procedure on how you set master schedules. They will then focus on your purchasing, quality, and engineering interface. Your purchasing employees must be well versed in your supplier procurement process, the methods used to survey your suppliers, the materials being brought into your operation, and the communication of changes with the supplier. After they are satisfied they will head out to your material handling areas. Ensure that your employees know their procedures and materials. For example, if you call for handling with electrostatic discharge bags, the employees need to be able to differentiate them from regular plastic bags and need to be wearing a discharge device when they handle the materials. If a material is considered defective, ensure that it is maintained in a separate flow and that all employees can recognize it as nonconforming material.

Upon completion of the materials areas the auditors will go to incoming inspection looking for continuity between engineering and purchasing as well as the usual competence and records. After they have sufficiently covered all of the key points they will confer among themselves. You will probably already know the verdict, but they will officially tell you at the exit interview. If you pass, congratulations for achieving certification on the first audit. It is a major accomplishment, and you will be proud to display your certificate prominently (see Figure 4.9).

Where do the auditors usually find problems? One of the leading QS-9000 auditors shared his perspective with us on where he usually finds a problem on the first audit:

- Customer drawing being reviewed in a timely manner (4.5).
- External documents being controlled properly (4.5).
- Training as a strategic initiative (4.18).
- Special characteristics didn't make it into the control plan (4.2.3).
- The manual says they will use FMEA according to the AIAG manual but they don't define the RPN number for action (4.2.3).
- MSA method not defined in manual (4.11.4).
- Engineering and actual implementation dates not recorded (4.5.2).
- Lack of supplier evaluations (4.6.2).
- Not requesting 100% on-time delivery (4.15.6).
- Failure to maintain governmental permits (4.16).
- No improvement plans around Ppk and Cpk assessments (2.3 (Section II)).
- Gage status not recording as found as well as left (4.11.3).

DNV Certification, Inc.

DET NORSKE VERITAS
QUALITY SYSTEM CERTIFICATE

Certificate No. 96-HOU-AQ-8351

This is to certify that the Quality System
of

SPAN INSTRUMENTS, INC.

at

2201 Avenue K, Plano, TX 75074 USA

Has been found to conform to Quality Standard:

ISO 9001, 1994
and the requirements of:
QS 9000, 1995
and has been audited in accordance with the requirements of:
QS-9000 Appendix B, Code of Practice

This Certificate is valid for the following products/service ranges:

DESIGN AND MANUFACTURE OF PROCESS CONTROL INSTRUMENTATION

Place and date:		This certificate is valid until:
Houston, Texas; 05 June 1996		23 May 1999

for the Accredited Unit:
Det Norske Veritas Certification, Inc.
Houston, Texas, USA
DNV Management System Certification
The Netherlands

Initial Certification Date:

23 May 1996

Garnett Davis
Management Representative
DNV Certification, Inc.

Accredited by
the RvA

Doug Sutton
Lead Auditor

Lack of fulfillment of conditions as set out in the Appendix may render this certificate invalid.

DET NORSKE VERITAS CERTIFICATION, INC., 16340 Park Ten Place, Suite 100, Houston, TX 77084 USA TEL: (713) 579-9003 FAX: (713) 647-2842

FIGURE 4.9.   Span's QS-9000 certification.

These are a few areas that you might want to add to your auditor's doublecheck list!

If you fail the first time, you are in good company. Your challenge will be to salvage as much of the positive audit as possible and arrange with the auditors for a revisit, quickly. Each registrar has its own approach, and it is best to clarify this early on and press the agents to live up to their earlier promises. If the audit goes badly initially, don't let them stop there—keep them going for two reasons. First, you need the visibility, and second, your organization needs the exposure. You will pay more, but it will be worth it. If you recall, you thought you were ready before the audit and without the auditor's visibility and their exposure to your management it is most likely that you will have another bad experience, unless something changes. After two bad experiences you could be putting your career in jeopardy, as management will usually opt for a new team and coach.

Hopefully, you will have a positive audit and hold a celebration to congratulate the entire company—everyone will have earned it. Eventually the certificate comes in and all is forgiven, but hopefully not forgotten. There is still the distinct possibility that when the auditors come back to close out some questionable findings, you could stumble, even though you had passed the first time. The other point is to realize that they will be back every six months (some auditors only every 12 months) to perform another shorter but more rigorous and in-depth audit focused on a specific operation. Passing these regular audits ensures continued QS-9000 certification and causes you to get even better.

If one of your customers lodges a complaint against your operations, the auditor is likely to investigate the complaint at the next audit, or if the complaint is serious enough, you may be required to move up the regularly scheduled audit.

TANGIBLE RETURNS

After almost a full year of pursuing our world-class phased manufacturing strategy and living within the certified QS-9000 process for better than 6 months, the following results have occurred:

- Profits: Span moved from losing money to double-digit profit-ability.
- On-Time Delivery: From the 50 percent realm into the high 90th percentile.
- Product Lead Times: Down from 22 weeks to 4.
- Warranty Claims: Reduced by more than 50 percent.
- Rework: Reduced by more than 50 percent.
- Out of Box Audit nonconformances: From 480,000 Ppm to less than 10,000 Ppm. (The OBA number is a measure representing any nonconformance. Our customers very rarely see these types of nonconformances.)
- Customer Satisfaction Indexes: Increase from previously 60 percent to the high 90s.
- Purchasing Cost Savings: Net 5 percent reduction in total purchased items.
- Scrap: Reduced by more than 50 percent.
- New Products: A clearly defined stream of new products in process, with cross-functional teams that believe in the process and aggressively work together.

These results were not because of QS-9000. Instead, QS-9000 established a format and set of expectations that the organization met. The real success came from the employees and management working together all focusing on a level of performance and utilizing various tools to get there. QS-9000 was the road map!

These results also allowed Span to enter into a very friendly merger with the publicly traded Tylan General Corporation, where all parties benefited. The Tylan General Corporation has seen these results and now QS-9000 is part of the corporate plan to migrate all their operations to compliance and certification.

5

What Do They Really Mean?

At times you will read the standard and say, "What do they really mean?" This chapter examines the elements of the QS-9000 standard as an auditor might. It rephrases the QS-9000 standard elements by section, clarifying and augmenting each area and addressing the questions that would likely arise in reading the sections.

Wherever "shall, must, or required" is mentioned in the standard, you can be reasonably sure that an auditor will ask you for objective evidence demonstrating your level of compliance. Descriptions of what must be in place to satisfy the "shall" requirements are listed following the explanation of each section of this chapter.

It should also be noted that when the standard says "documented," there are numerous methods of documentation as well as formats. However, no matter what these documents look like, the standard requires that they be under some form of revision control and be maintained. Documents also have a generic meaning in that they refer to work instructions, assembly drawings, test instructions, test parameters, or just about any instructional vehicle used to communicate how an operation ought to be performed, with regard to the satisfaction of a customer requirement.

SECTION ONE: ISO 9000-BASED REQUIREMENTS

The QS-9000, Section 1 of the standard focuses on 20 aspects of a quality program that are subject to a rigorous audit during the certification process. Each section relates to a specific aspect of satisfying customers. When trying to determine how each section applies to your organization, ask yourself how it relates to your customer's expectations.

The following 20 elements are contained in Section 1 of the QS-9000 standard document:

- 4.1 Management Responsibility.
- 4.2 Quality System.
- 4.3 Contract Review.
- 4.4 Design Control.
- 4.5 Document and Data Control.
- 4.6 Purchasing.
- 4.7 Control of Customer Supplied Product.
- 4.8 Product Identification and Traceability.
- 4.9 Process Control.
- 4.10 Inspection and Testing.
- 4.11 Control of Inspection, Measuring, and Test Equipment.
- 4.12 Inspection and Test Status.
- 4.13 Control of Nonconforming Product.
- 4.14 Corrective and Preventive Action.
- 4.15 Handling, Storage, Packaging, Preservation, and Delivery.
- 4.16 Control of Quality Records.
- 4.17 Internal Quality Audits.
- 4.18 Training.
- 4.19 Servicing.
- 4.20 Statistical Techniques.

The details associated with each of these elements are discussed in the following sections.

4.1 Management Responsibility

Deming, Juran, and other quality experts believed that management was primarily responsible for 80 percent to 90 percent of an organization's problems. Appropriately, management responsibility is the first element of the QS-9000 standard.

4.1.1 Quality Policy.

Management must define and document its quality policy and objectives to ensure its commitment to quality and to the minimum requirements of QS-9000. Management must see that this policy is understood and implemented throughout the organization and ensure that:

- The quality policy is defined and documented.
- The quality policy is relevant to your customers' needs.
- The policy is known by everyone in your organization.
- The policy is maintained and implemented at all levels in your organization.

4.1.2 Organization.

This subsection requires you to be able to prove that the template for your organization's quality approach is effective and defines responsibility. The standard calls for you to address problems systematically and solve them by attacking the root causes.

Specifically, you must be certain that:

- You have defined and documented who has responsibility to stop the processing or delivery when a deficiency is detected.
- You have clearly defined who has the authority to identify and record deficiencies, recommend solutions, and verify their correction.
- You have allocated trained resources to conduct verification (i.e., audits) of your quality system.
- A senior member of your organization has been assigned responsibility for the QS-9000 standard and your organization's compliance as well as for reporting its status to the organization.

4.1.2.1 Responsibility and Authority.

An authority must be identified who can manage and verify that work affecting quality is performed as documented by your quality system. This person must have the freedom and authority to ensure the organization addresses and prevents nonconforming activities, maintains records of quality problems, and causes the organization to correct the nonconformity. This individual later investigates and verifies that the solution has succeeded. He or she must also be able to stop the operation or a shipment if required and report it appropriately. Most companies provide an organization chart, with a path from the president down through the line personnel, with designated individuals having specific responsibilities for quality control or quality assurance.

4.1.2.2 Resources.

Management must maintain an in-house verification capacity for the primary purpose of conducting an internal audit. Audit personnel must be adequately trained for verification activities (see 4.17, Internal Audits and 4.18, Training).

Internal auditors are required to verify that your entire operation conforms to your quality plan as well as to all the elements of QS-9000. These audits need to be carried out on a regular basis (at least once per year) to ensure compliance. Regular means that your organization should be prepared to be audited by a third party at any given time with a high probability of passing.

The dynamics of your process and common industry practice dictate the interval of your audits. Audits as described in this section must be carried out by a trained, independent party that is not immediately responsible for the area being audited.

These audits need to carry the appropriate level of documentation. You must prove to the third-party auditors that they were carried out as part of an overall comprehensive plan for the audit of the organization and that they are rigorous in nature (i.e., you will be required to show comment and actions).

4.1.2.3 Management Representative.

A senior management representative must be designated to ensure that the requirements of QS-9000 and all other defined quality standards are established and maintained. This also includes ensuring that all the organizational interfaces are appropriately involved in the Advanced Product Quality Planning and Control Plan, with regard to product development, introduction, and ongoing production. This management representative ensures that there is a multidisciplinary team approach being used, where regular communication is maintained.

People who are designated as the quality contacts can have multiple functions within your organization; therefore, it is not necessary that they have a strictly quality-related title. However, you need to be careful of the fox-in-the-henhouse syndrome. It is quite possible that your senior production manager within the manufacturing organization is responsible for total quality in his organization, including the verification and inspection aspects. If so, there needs to be a very strong case made, supported by documented evidence, that this individual is knowledgeable, acting impartially, and meeting the full intent of the standard. An easy way to define the quality responsibility is to designate quality responsibilities from the president to the assemblyline person on your corporate organization chart.

• You will use a multidisciplinary team for decision making.

4.1.3 Management Review.

The management of your organization must regularly review the results of the entire quality system (not just ISO) to determine that it is doing the intended job. This review should be based on measures that include the internal audit data and customer feedback as well as appropriate incremental quality improvement data indicating the overall effectiveness of your system. You must document these reviews, and they should occur regularly or when an indicator reveals an undesirable result. Having an active quality council continually upgrading your operations and recording these meetings and upgrades effectively serves this requirement.

4.1.4 Business Plan.

Your organization is required to maintain a business plan that extends at least 3 years. The plan should cover the typical business planning areas: finance, marketing and sales, product development, manufacturing support, quality plans, and customer satisfaction goals. This should include a series of key business measures collected at regular intervals and tracked and communicated to the appropriate members within the organization for comparison to your plan. You will also have to demonstrate how you track and update your plan. (Your business plan content is not subject to the auditors' review, however you must demonstrate that it does exist.)

• You shall have a business plan with document reviews.

4.1.5 Analysis and Use of Company-Level Data.

Your organization will have to establish measures and trends identifying your progress in attaining your business plan. This would also include benchmarking your competitors' performance as well as looking at your customers' problems. As appropriate, a prioritized list of potential actions should be developed.

- You shall have documented trends in quality, performance, and productivity.

4.1.6 Customer Satisfaction.

You need a documented process that regularly creates objective and valid measures with trends of customer satisfaction. A comparison of competitor and industry benchmarks needs to be shared with senior management.

- You shall have a documented process for determining customer satisfaction.

4.2 Quality System

4.2.1 General.

The intention of this element is to ensure that you define, document, and maintain your quality system in a way that results in satisfaction of your customer's expectations. This means that you must have a manual that incorporates the QS-9000 standard and also references the procedures that you are using to meet the standard.

In summary, the standard states that:

- You will have a quality manual that defines your quality system.
- Your manual shall include references to documented procedures that form your quality system.

4.2.2 Quality System Procedures.

You must prepare documented and controlled procedures that meet the QS-9000 and any other relevant requirements. For example, if you are telling your customers that you are meeting Good Manufacturing Practices (GMP) or military standards, then your procedures and manual should reflect it.

It goes without saying that your actual practices should meet your defined procedures. But how much do you have to document? There is no easy answer; it is a balance between the task's effect on the quality of the product, the complexity, and the level of recorded training that you have provided beforehand. An excellent training program can significantly reduce your documented procedural load.

To adequately address this clause:

- You must have the appropriate quality procedures that meet the QS-9000 standard, and your activities must be conducted in accordance with your procedures.

4.2.3 Quality Planning.

The establishment of a documented quality plan is a required element. Contrary to ISO 9000, where the specification is fairly open, the QS-9000 standard requires you follow the Advanced Product Quality Planning and Control Plan (APQP) reference manual with regard to product planning. Auditors look for a cross-functional team to be leading this effort. The team must develop a control plan that closely mimics the APQP and covers the three distinct phases of a product's life (prototype, prelaunch, and production). During the audit you will be required to step a product through the APQP with appropriate back-up to the phases. To help your effort, you might also consider going a step further and defining your quality plan via a relationship diagram—that is, groups of boxes (functions) that connect to other boxes, with descriptions of the relationship. This diagram should reference where your quality plans come from, where your in-process controls are established, where inspection equipment is defined, where production resources and training are determined, and where design review is developed as well as the test procedures, who establishes the quality control techniques, points of inspection, and measures required for process capabilities, test and verification. The plan needs to address who will be responsible for the clarification of the standards for acceptance as well as how records are generated, their contents, and how they are kept.

Once you have all the relationships determined, develop an APQP checklist with a "Who should be involved" list of each phase. This control plan shall be considered a live document and will be updated to incorporate any changes in the product content, processes used to build the product, or when the process becomes incapable or unstable.

This element also calls for a feasibility review prior to accepting a customer order for a proposed product.

In your quality planning effort:

- You must document how you intend to meet the product, contract, and project quality requirements.
- You will utilize the APQP, which requires a cross-functional team to develop a control plan for the product. The team will address: the customers' needs, designs, failure modes and effects of the product and process, development of processes and capabilities, acquisition of equipment, human resource skills, capacity, service support, suitable verification points during the production process, needed quality checkpoints, quality records, and the eventual production of the product and continuation of improvement.
- You will have controls for all special characteristics.
- You will have feasibility reviews prior to accepting an order to build a product.

4.3 Contract Review

4.3.1 General.

Your organization must have a systematic and documented method for ensuring that you understand and can meet your customers' needs. If your specifications differ from your customer requirements, there must be an orderly method for reconciliation. You also must have a way to ensure that you have adequate capacity to meet the combined needs of all customers, if applicable. The QS-9000 standard also suggests that communications be maintained with the customer during the life of the order as appropriate.

This clause seeks to ensure that:

- You have documented procedures for the input and review of your customers' orders.

4.3.2 Review.

You are required to review your customers' orders prior to accepting them via a defined communications channel. To be considered effective, you must first achieve a complete understanding of what they are requesting. The standard indicates a preference for a written order, but the authors of QS-9000 understand that a verbal order is fairly common. In this case, they ask you to put a methodology in place that ensures the verbal order is confirmed and agreed to at the time of acceptance. When you receive the order, you must make sure you can honor it in all respects. This would include such items as special characteristics unique to the customer and its contract.

Therefore, you must confirm that:

- The customer's order is well documented or well understood if verbally given prior to accepting the order.
- You have the capability to meet the order, and all discrepancies are resolved prior to the order.

4.3.3 Amendment to Contract.

On occasion your customer may change its order, or worse yet, you may not be able to meet your original commitment. You must have a documented system in place that defines how you go about communicating and executing these changes with your customer as well as your own internal organization.

The standard states that:

- You must show a documented system of how you make changes to an order and methods employed to ensure the information is correctly transferred to all the affected parties.

4.3.4 Records.

Upon review of a customer order by an authorized person, a record of the order and the review must be maintained.

- You must maintain a record of the customer's order for an appropriately defined period of time.

4.4 Design Control

4.4.1 General.

This section requires you to maintain a documented process for the design of your product that produces the performance characteristics you promise your customers. This element of the standard applies only to those companies that are responsible for the design. A puzzling question arises when you contribute to a small proportion of the design. If you perform a final sign-off, you are responsible for the complete design. Discuss this point with your customer and ensure that the interpretation is fully understood.

- You must have documented procedures to ensure the designs of your products meet your customers' requirements.

4.4.2 Design and Development Planning.

This design plan must define how the design process will be carried out. It encompasses all levels of staff involved, their communications, and process paths. The design process must undergo regular and documented management reviews by approved personnel who have a minimum set of required skills to carry out an effective design review. Those in charge of design control must staff the function with appropriately trained people and equipment. The design group should contain individuals who are appropriately trained in the following skills: geometric dimensioning and tolerencing, quality function deployment, design for manufacturing, design for assembly, design of experiments, failure mode and effects analysis for both the process and design, finite element analysis, solid modeling, simulation techniques, computer-aided design, computer-aided engineering, and reliability engineering. While you don't have to have expertise in all the elements, you will need to demonstrate strength in those areas that affect your products.
   To accomplish this:

- You must have a documented plan for every design.
- This plan must define who is qualified to perform the designs and the qualified resources needed.

- The plan must be updated at your defined milestones as you evolve the design and reference the appropriate tools required to ensure a good design.

4.4.3 Organizational and Technical Interfaces.

All technical interfaces between the designer and other organizations required to design a product need to be identified, communicated with, and reviewed by the interfaces regularly. These may include marketing, sales, manufacturing, legal, and product safety. The information required for the design process from other organizations (input requirements) must also be defined.

Therefore:

- Your plan should define from whom you must receive information and guidance as well as the information to be received.

4.4.4 Design Input.

You must have a defined system to ensure all appropriate design requirements are received by the design group whether they are performed by your organization or subcontracted to an outside source. This includes all customer and regulatory requirements. A listing of specifications and unique characteristics of the product must be maintained. The design group must actively communicate, detail, and resolve inconsistencies in the product requirements. This communication assumes two-way communications via your CAD/CAE system. (If you don't have a computer-aided design or engineering system, you will need a waiver from your customer).

This communication effort is designed to:

- Ensure your designs meet all applicable regulatory requirements and provide supporting documentation.
- Resolve design ambiguities with the input source.
- Ensure your design input plans and reviews document the customer contract requirements where appropriate.
- You will have computer-aided design and engineering capabilities.

4.4.5 Design Output.

The output of the design process includes documented drawings, test requirements and tolerance requirements, materials specifications, appropriate assembly instructions, and test methodologies. Design output is to be documented and expressed in terms of requirements, calculations, and analyses. This output will also specifically reference all the appropriate regulatory or association standards and any critical requirements to the design that relate to the safe assembly and operation of the product.

As a supplement, this element requires that the output included efforts to simplify, optimize, and innovate and to reduce waste and use all the tools identified in the design development. In addition, cost performance and risk trade-offs shall be considered in the design. Use of feedback from testing, production and field failure reports shall all be considered in the final output.

This clause seeks to ensure that:

- The design characteristics are documented in such a form as they can be verified.
- The design characteristics meet the design inputs as well as contain acceptance criteria and integrate efforts to simplify, inovate and reduce waste as well as utilize the tools described in the APQP.
- The design review ensures that unique requirements such as handling, storage, and safe operation are included as part of the output.

4.4.6 Design Review.

You must perform design reviews at defined stages of product development. You need to define what is involved at each stage and who needs to be involved at that particular stage. This means that at some point during the design, you must invite all those you have identified to approve of the design (4.4.3). Their acceptance must be recorded and maintained.

Therefore:

- At your defined design review stages, you must have records that show participation by those operations required for the review.
- The design review must include documented input as well as output.

4.4.7 Design Verification.

You must conduct a formal and documented verification of the product design to ensure that all defined criteria are satisfied. This design verification should include qualification testing, comparison with a similar design, or any other calculation that will enable you to ensure that you meet the design input requirements. These verification measures must be recorded and retained along with the design verification acceptance.

As a supplement to this element a comprehensive prototype must be developed, and product reliability and durability testing shall be conducted. When possible, the products being tested will come from the same production process intended to provide the product on an ongoing basis. Testing will be tracked and monitored to ensure that all requirements are met and completed to schedule.

While not specifically stated in the standard, we strongly recommend making use of the Production Part Approval Process (PPAP) reference manual with regard to the process requirements and evaluations considered necessary for submission for approval.

Design verification specifies that:

- As your designs evolve, they must be verified to ensure the inputs are being met prior to release.
- Designs are verified via tests, calculations, demonstrations, and comparisons with previously proven designs, and all methods used have the appropriate supportive documentation.
- That you engage in a formal prototype program.

4.4.8 Design Validation.

You need to ensure the final product meets the design input, which should be the same as the customer's requirements. This validation should occur in the same environment for which the product is intended. If you have multiple environments and intended uses, it should be tested for all of them. The product must meet the full requirements.

Consult the PPAP to ensure that you have covered all the approval requirements, thus improving your chances for an approved submission.

To achieve design validation:

- The product shall be tested in its expected operating environment following design verification to ensure it meets customers' requirements.

4.4.9 Design Changes.

The process for making changes to your design should be documented. The routine should essentially meet the same criteria as those for a new design with all the appropriate reviews and authorized signatures.

As a supplement to this element, any design changes must have customer approval prior to implementation or a customer waiver. The automotive suppliers are sensitive to any changes to the form, fit, function, performance, and durability and therefore require prior communications.

When you make a design change:

- You must have a documented system that accommodates identification of the change and a review by those involved and affected by the change, and you must show approval by the authorized individuals.
- Your change process must include customer notification and approval prior to implementation of the change.

(See Chapter 7 for more information with regard to the APQP.)

4.5 Document and Data Control

4.5.1 General.

All documents that are pertinent to the QS-9000 standard must be under some type of formal documentation control, with procedures defining their establishment, review, upgrade, authorization, and removal upon obsolescence. They may be in any media format that is desired as long as they are available at their point of use and understood by those using the documents.

This includes external reference documents used in areas such as design and testing. When a customer indicates a process is critical to the form, fit, function, performance, or safety, they will deem it as a special characteristic and will appropriately give it a symbol or notation. Your documentation will also carry this symbol, notation, or your company's equivalent.

- You must have a documented system in place to ensure that the control of all documents, instructions, and data in your system meet QS-9000 requirements.
- Customer drawings or specifications must be appropriately available at all points of use and marked with the customer's special characteristics markings.

4.5.2 Documentation and Data Approval and Issue.

All your documents and data must require approval by an authorized person. This means that you must formally authorize individuals and they must be capable of assessing the adequacy of the document. You will then have to maintain a master list of all the documents being used (including your customer supplied engineering documents) and their appropriate revision status and a documentation control procedure that identifies how you maintain all procedures. This listing or procedure is required to ensure that only current revision documents are being used and that all obsolete documents are removed. The current documents must be available at their point of use, and if for some reason you require that the old documents be available, they must be properly identified as not intended for current use. As these revisions are implemented in production, an implementation date must be recorded and retained. When a customer provides an updated revision to a document, it must be reviewed within days of receipt.

To comply with this clause:

- All the documents that are used must be reviewed and approved by the authorized personnel.
- You must have a listing of all currently active documents that are available to those using them.
- You must ensure that only current and authorized documents are available for use.

- Instructional documents must be available where the lack thereof could adversely affect the quality of the product being produced.
- Obsolete or incorrect documents must be removed from those areas where they could be used. If there is a need to retain such documents, they must be appropriately identified as being for information purposes only.
- Production as well as engineering implementation dates must be recorded.
- You must have a procedure for the prompt review and update of customer documents.

4.5.3 Document Changes.

Any changes made to the documentation require the same review and authorization that the establishment of the original document requires. When possible, an overview of the change to the document should be included with the new release. Changes to prior documents should be noted to assist those working with the document.

Document changes:

- Must be reviewed and approved by those who performed the initial review or by a designated individual who has access to the pertinent data to ensure a sound decision.
- New changes from the prior documents will be outlined, when at all possible.

4.6 Purchasing

4.6.1 General.

You are required to conduct your purchasing operations in a systematic fashion that ensures you are obtaining the proper materials for the organization's specified requirements. When a customer has approved a particular subcontractor, you may add a new subcontractor only with the permission of the customer's materials engineering group.

All the materials used to manufacture a part shall meet or exceed all local governmental regulations with regard to the environment and safety.

Compliance with this clause requires that:

- You will develop and demonstrate a working purchasing system with full documentation and records that ensures your purchased materials meet your specifications and, if appropriate, your customers'.
- If your customer has provided or approved your supplier, you may buy only from the approved supplier.
- You may buy materials only from suppliers who meet all governmental regulations.

4.6.2 Evaluation of Subcontractors.

Assessment of a supplier must include a formal documented review methodology. The organization must maintain the assessment records of a supplier and a formal documented listing of suppliers who meet this approved process. This approved supplier listing must be available to those using it.

The supplier evaluation process used to determine acceptability is based on the type of product being secured, past experience with the supplier, and its capabilities. In all cases, the assessment must specify the quality of the materials received. You must maintain records of the supplier's evaluation as well as the acceptability of the materials received and delivery performance. A somewhat misunderstood fact is that your suppliers do not have to be certified to the QS-9000 or ISO 9000 standard; however, your evaluation of the supplier must be based upon sections 1 and 2 of the QS-9000 standard and you are required to assist your suppliers with the development of their quality system. Your organization will have to carry out regular assessments of the supplier or you may use an accredited third-party registrar or your customer's evaluation to satisfy the need for supplier assessment. On occasion the customer will designate a supplier for your use. This does not relieve you of the obligation to ensure the quality of parts and services.

The standard requires that you set your supplier on-time delivery goal at 100 percent. It also requires that you provide them with the necessary planning information and commitments to ensure they can meet the 100 percent on-time goal. You will also have to track how well your suppliers are meeting your goal. You will have to identify any premium handling or freight costs and take some form of corrective action to reduce these costs.

Evaluation of subcontractors requires that:

- You systematically select a supplier on their ability to meet your quality requirements.
- You include an evaluation of their quality systems based upon QS-9000.
- You must define how you will ensure that every purchased part and supplier is evaluated.
- You maintain accessible records of your acceptable suppliers (i.e., an approved vendor list).
- Establish a system for the tracking of supplier on-time delivery performance.
- You require 100 percent on-time delivery from your suppliers and you provide them with the information and commitments needed to meet this goal.

4.6.3 Purchasing Data.

The material being purchased must be fully described. This includes specific part identification. You must also describe process requirements, inspection instructions, special markings, and any other detailed information relevant to the acceptance of the material.

The purchase document must include notation of compliance to any relevant standard (QS-9000 is one of those standards). Prior to the release of the specification requirement to the supplier, an appropriately trained individual must review it to ensure adequacy. This individual can be the originator of the requirement. With regard to restrictive substances, you must maintain a process by which your organization monitors all toxic and hazardous material and ensures that all governmental requirements are met.

To satisfy this clause:

- Your purchasing data must contain a clear description of the product desired.
- The data must incorporate all relevant information regarding composition, form, process requirements, and inspection instructions as well as the quality standard to be applied.

- You must review and approve the purchasing document for all relevant data prior to release.
- Your organization must have a system in place to control hazardous or restricted substances.

4.6.4.1 and 4.6.4.2 Verification of Purchased Product.

It is the purchaser's option to perform a source inspection of the product (at your supplier's location) or to perform the inspection on the purchaser's site. In either case, inspection location does not absolve the supplier of the responsibility to inspect and fully comply with its own quality policy, as described to the purchaser. If the purchaser provides for source inspection at the supplier's site, the purchaser does not surrender the right to reject the material at any later time. If you decide to perform a source inspection, it must be noted on your purchase order to the supplier.

Product verification seeks to ensure that:

- When you perform source inspections (i.e., inspect at the supplier's location), the arrangement must be specified in the purchasing document.

4.7 Control of Customer-Supplied Product

You must establish procedures for the inspection, storage, handling, and maintenance of materials, packaging and equipment provided to you by your customer. Should this material become unusable for any reason, it must be segregated, identified, and reported to your customer.

This could be considered a mirror policy of your expectations and policies for the proper handling of your own materials. Your supplier's unique expectations will be defined in the initial contract, and procedures will be required to support such activities.

The following steps are required for the control of customer-supplied product:

- When your customer provides you with material for use, you must have a documented system in place that guarantees you will handle their materials as you would your own, within your

QS-9000-compliant system. This would include packaging materials and tooling.
- Should you lose or render any of the customer's material unusable, it must be reported to the customer.

4.8 Product Identification and Traceability

You must maintain procedures for the proper identification and documentation of materials as they move through the production, installation, and delivery processes to ensure that the customer's requirements are satisfied.

Depending on your customer's requirements, you also may need to address production lot identification or component traceability. The standard says this is to be done "where appropriate," meaning as required by your customer or where it is not inherently obvious. Your customer may request that your product have varying degrees of traceability. You must ensure there are formal and documented methods and records in place to satisfy this request.

To maintain product identification and traceability:

- You must have a documented system for ensuring the materials are uniquely identified from the moment they arrive to the point of customer receipt.
- If contracted by your customers or required by regulatory bodies or you have determined that material traceability is desired, you must have a documented system that records the appropriate information to achieve this objective.

4.9 Process Control

Process control refers to the entire process of producing a product and the method by which you control and ensure that your processes are followed—it is not limited to some form of statistical process control. The standard frequently uses the term *procedures* when referring to process control.

You must provide a controlled work environment that ensures that the quality of the product is adequate and in conformance with the documentation and record requirements of QS-9000. This controlled environment will also meet all governmental and environmental regulations and as appropriate, you will be required to produce the appropriate documents as evidence of compliance.

You will need to provide adequate and controlled written instructions (i.e., procedures or work instructions) or representative samples that ensure proper assembly and workmanship standards. These standards should define the criteria for acceptable workmanship.

The process should define the equipment, environment, reference standards, and quality plans and must include regular monitoring during production. The equipment used by the employees must have appropriate operating instructions and maintenance plans.

Work instructions must be reviewed by authorized personnel. These instructions are required whenever their absence could adversely affect the quality of the output. The instructions should be reviewed periodically to ensure adequacy and proper alignment with other procedures. The work instructions must clearly define the acceptance criteria so the operator can differentiate the good from the bad.

A special process is any process that cannot be fully confirmed through immediate testing or inspection such that a defect may surface only when the product is being used by the customer. Typical examples are welding, paint applications, and heat treatment of materials. These processes require identification as special processes, clearly defined process parameters, operation by appropriately trained personnel using qualified equipment, and/or continuous monitoring with supporting records. Special processes must also meet the full requirements of this section.

To assure that your operations run to the schedules committed to your customers, you must engage in a formal preventive maintenance program. This program must establish procedures and maintenance schedules for the maintenance of the key process equipment. The preventive program should attempt to adopt predictive maintenance methods and be supported with a replacement parts plan.

To meet the requirements of this section:

- You must have a documented and controlled system of procedures and instructions in place that ensures all processes affecting customer requirements and special characteristics are carried out in a controlled manner.

- Documented procedures are required where the lack thereof could adversely affect the quality of the product or service being provided.
- A controlled process should include the approval of suitable production, installation, and servicing equipment by an authorized individual.
- Appropriate process and product requirements shall be monitored during the processing of the customer's requirements.
- A suitable working environment and maintenance program for your equipment shall be provided for.
- Clear accept or reject decision criteria shall be documented and made available, as related to workmanship or material conformance.
- When you cannot immediately verify acceptability of the material or workmanship (termed special processes, such as painting, welding, and heat treating) you must identify prequalified process parameters and provide fully trained personnel and authorized equipment. The documentation must also include a full identification of all special processes and ensure continual process parameter monitoring of those processes.

4.9.1 Process Monitoring and Operator Instructions.

All operations require a method for monitoring performance against a documented standard available at the workstation. The standard suggests that you review the Advanced Product Quality Planning and Control (APQP) reference manual for the appropriate monitoring controls and instructions. The monitoring should use some form of process sheet, inspection, or lab report. The instructions should carry the following as appropriate: operation name and number, part names and numbers, current engineering revision, tools and gauges, material disposition instructions, customer supplier special characteristics, SPC requirements, engineering standards, inspection and test instructions, corrective actions, revision data approvals, visual aids, and tool change intervals.

- You shall prepare document monitoring instructions.

4.9.2 Preliminary Process Capability.

Before you begin regular production of the product you must engage in a preliminary process capability study. The processes should meet what the standard calls a Ppk of 1.6 unless otherwise requested by the customer. (Think of this as a process capability study, only established before you begin regular production.) Should you have any questions with regard to the calculation, consult the Statistical Process Control (SPC) reference manual. The Production Part Approval Process (PPAP) should be referenced when the process fails to meet the 1.6 criteria (section V.D. Preliminary Process Capability Studies). Those processes that fail to meet these requirements shall require a corrective action involving mistake-proofing. Attribute data shall be used to prioritize improvements; however, it cannot be used as part of this statistical study. All processes shall have a continuous improvement plan in place (especially for those processes yielding unacceptable results).

- You shall prepare preliminary process capability instructions around customer-designated special characteristics.
- This study shall meet the requirements outlined in the PPAP.

4.9.3 Ongoing Process Performance Requirements.

Once your production process has begun, a stable process must maintain a Cpk of 1.33 unless otherwise requested by your customer. Unstable processes shall have an output greater than 1.67 Ppk. When a process does not support normal data, other methods will be required and agreed upon by the customer.

Significant changes to the process must be noted on the control. You may make revisions to the control plan due to high capability indexes, provided you have your customer's approval prior to changing the plan.

Where characteristics of the process fail to meet the criteria, a 100 percent inspection plan must be invoked along with a corrective action plan. In some instances these plans must be reviewed with the customer. All processes shall have a continuous improvement plan in place, with the greatest emphasis placed upon special characteristics.

- Significant process events will be noted on the control charts.

4.9.4 Modified or Preliminary Ongoing Capability Requirements.

A customer may determine that a higher or lower process capability is desired. You will have to modify the control plan as per the customer's request.

4.9.5 Verification of Job Set-Ups.

Job set-ups must be documented and confirmed to meet all requirements. Where possible, attempt to use statistical verification.

- Job set-ups must be documented and verified.

4.9.6 Process Changes.

Generally, when a production process, engineering level, location, material source, or process environment is changed, prior approval must be received from the customer as defined in the PPAP. Guidance on this matter is best discussed with the customer in advance as the customer does not want to slow your continuous improvement efforts.

- You shall maintain the dates of the process changes.

4.9.7 Appearance Items.

Where a part's appearance is considered critical, the supplier will assure that masters of color texture and grain are controlled and that appropriate lighting for evaluation is available. The employees must also be trained and qualified (you don't need a color-blind person matching colors).

- If you manufacture appearance items you will comply with this element.

4.10 Inspection and Testing

4.10.1 General.

This element deals with the testing of your materials as they move through your processes as well as the final inspection of the product.

The testing operations must be carried out in accordance with your documented procedures and supported with records that indicate the status of the material and eventual satisfactory status of all requirements prior to the product's release. The acceptance criteria for your testing of attribute data should require a "$c = 0$" (no rejects found) approach, where no defects are allowed. When testing is performed by an outside laboratory, the lab must be identified by a nationally recognized accreditation body, unless otherwise approved by your customer.

This element also deals with emergency situations that occur in real life. For example, the standard allows you to release incoming materials for urgent production without inspection. However, if you bypass inspection, you must employ a positive recall procedure. This procedure requires that you track this material and be able to identify it, should further testing indicate that your materials or workmanship is unsatisfactory.

To comply with this clause:

- You must maintain a documented inspection and testing system to ensure the customer's requirements are met. This activity must be supported by accessible records that show compliance.
- Should you have an emergency requirement that prevents screening for fitness, you must establish a unique material identity that must be recorded and tracked as it moves through your processes should the need for a recall occur (i.e., a positive recall procedure).
- The positive recall procedure will not apply to final inspection.
- Your attribute sampling plan must be set at $c = 0$.
- You must use accredited laboratores.

4.10.2 Receiving Inspection and Testing.

No material should be incorporated into the product without verification to the product specifications. This does not mean all your material must undergo a full specification inspection. You may use one or more of the following methods to meet these requirements: receipt of statistical data, receiving inspection using a sampling plan based upon performance, second- or third-part assessments at a subcontractor's location, subcontractor's warrant of certification (with test results).

If, due to an emergency, the incoming material is used without verification, it will require designated authorization, full documentation, and tracking (i.e., a positive recall procedure). All preverified materials should be maintained in a segregated area according to a documented process.

The verification of the incoming product must conform to your quality plan and to documented procedures. Verification can take many acceptable forms and is not necessarily delegated to the receiving inspection organization. However, records must be maintained to meet the defined inspection requirements specified in your procedures. When establishing inspection schemes you should consider recorded evidence of receipt histories as well as the process capability of the supplier.

To verify incoming product:

- You shall establish a documented system that ensures that no incoming material is used until its fitness has been verified to your defined quality.
- When establishing an inspection and testing consideration, you should consider recorded evidence of process compliance as well as historic evidence of compliance.

4.10.3 In-Process Inspection and Testing.

You must document your in-process inspection procedures and test points and carry out the defined inspections. The level of in-process inspection is determined by your own operations, and with the exception of special process inspections, there is no additional requirement.

If in-process inspection is required, you will need to provide holding points for nonconforming materials. The QS-9000 standard encourages the use of in-process inspection as a secondary approach for minimizing defects. The standard strongly encourages defect prevention as the primary vehicle for improvement. Some of the suggested methods are statistical process control (SPC), error-proofing, and visuals. The standard allows in-process inspections to act as part of the final inspection and testing if appropriate.

This clause requires that:

- You perform in-process test and inspection of the product according to the documented product specification requirements or to your own quality plan.
- You not allow materials to proceed through the process until they have met the test requirements.

4.10.4 Final Inspection and Testing.

You are required to perform a full inspection and test of your final product as specified in your quality plan and documented procedures. This full inspection and test must verify that the inspection data fully meet the specifications of the product, as defined by your quality plan. Final inspection should incorporate the results of previous inspections and their successful satisfaction of requirements. You are required to hold the product and defer its shipment or release until all inspections have been completed and the product has met all the specifications. Your inspection record should indicate who authorized the release of the product (of course, this person must be authorized to do so).

The standard addresses the issue of layout inspections when appropriate. A layout inspection is a full inspection of all the dimensions on a part as shown on the drawings and should be done annually unless otherwise specified by the customer. A functional verification should occur at defined intervals, and results of both the layout inspection and functional tests shall be made available to the customer upon request.

To satisfy this requirement:

- You must perform final inspection and test of the product according to the documented product specification requirements or to your own quality plan to ensure the product meets the customer's specified requirements.
- The final inspection shall include verification of satisfactory in-process inspections.
- No products or materials shall pass final inspection until all requirements have been satisfied and records completed and released by authorized individuals.
- You shall conduct functional tests and layout verifications on a regular basis.

4.10.5 Inspection and Test Records.

You must keep records to demonstrate that your product has met the testing requirements and that all the tests were conducted per your quality plan (also see section 4.16).

This clause requires that:

- You shall maintain a documented system that ensures that inspection and test records are retained and accessible, demonstrating successful final inspection and test by an identified authorized individual.

4.11 Control of Inspection, Measuring, and Test Equipment

4.11.1 General.

You must ensure the proper maintenance, review, and control of all of your test, calibration, and any other test equipment (including jigs, fixtures, templates, patterns, and software) as defined by your quality plan. This equipment must be capable of measuring to the level of accuracy specified in the test requirements. Your employees must have been trained in the use and proper applications of the equipment and they must understand the variations that this equipment and the people using it might generate. If your customers request the technical test data on your inspection equipment to conduct their own study to determine functional adequacy, it must be made available to them.

Compliance with this section requires that:

- You have a documented system that ensures the identification and correct calibration of all equipment used to perform testing and inspection of materials and products.
- When using test software to verify product fitness, it shall be regularly rechecked to ensure correctness.
- Records of calibration, verification, and accuracy shall be maintained and available for customer inspection.

4.11.2 Control Procedure.

To comply with this section of the standard, you must determine how you can systematically address your measurement equipment. Your organization must begin by identifying what measure is to be made, by what piece of equipment, and to what specific tolerances. The equipment must be capable of making the required measurements, and you must show some proof that you did assure that it was capable of making the measurements. Once you have identified the correct equipment you must define how you will calibrate all test equipment at regular intervals of time usage. The calibration of this equipment must be compared with a known good with a clear path to a nationally recognized standard. Calibration cycle times are usually based on the manufacturer's guidelines, or less often by history and usage. If there are no standards to reference, you must document how to meet your desired standard by defining your own. Your calibration system should call for the identification of the equipment to be used, where it is used, the method for confirmation, the frequency of inspection, and the procedure you will employ should it be found out of conformance. You will want to place some type of identification mark on the equipment to show its current calibration status. A set of calibration records will be maintained with the details of the calibration, maintenance or refurbishment if taken, and at least one available prior record. When a nonconformance trend is indicated, you must correct the nonconformance by shortening the calibration cycle or repairing or replacing a tool. Should the measurement device be determined to be outside of calibration, a range notification should also be sent to the usage point of the calibration equipment for reverification with a corrected tool. Be sure to properly store and maintain (through employee training) the calibration equipment. Permit only authorized personnel to make adjustments to the equipment or software.

Only the measurement and calibration equipment used in the final product test inspections or as defined in your quality plan is required to satisfy these requirements. If in-process inspections are used to validate requirements within the process, and they support your final inspection and testing activity, then the equipment must be made part of your calibration control scheme. Should you determine that a particular instrument is not required to meet the QS-9000 criteria, then you may exempt it by identifying it as such. However, from a good quality practice perspective, keeping as many pieces of equipment in compliance as possible to help you produce the best product at the lowest cost and achieve the goal of zero defects makes good sense. Third-party certification agents take a dim view if you try to stipulate that only your final test equipment needs calibration control. They will usually cite a failure in your corrective action process if you attempt to use this loophole. We advise that you discuss this with your auditor beforehand.

Consider the following checkpoints in you measurement and calibration control system:

- A review of the inspections and tests to be performed shall be identified and completed.
- You must identify and calibrate all your inspection and test equipment at defined and valid intervals to a national or international standard. When there is no such standard available, you must create your own documented standard.
- You must define how and when you will calibrate your equipment.
- You must define a reasonable course of action when you discover the equipment is out of calibration.
- There must be some form of identification on the calibrated equipment that would indicate its current status.
- You must maintain calibration records for each piece of equipment under calibration control.
- You must review the calibration records when the equipment is found to be out of calibration. From this review you will need to define a corrective action to minimize future nonconformances.
- Ensure that the working environment is conducive to effective testing.
- Ensure that the equipment is adequately protected and handled between calibration checks. This includes making sure there are no unauthorized adjustments to the equipment.

4.11.3 Inspection Measuring and Test Equipment Records.

Records of calibration verification must be kept for gauge conditions and actual readings at time of receipt for calibration. Should engineering changes occur affecting these instruments a record shall also be retained. Customer notification must occur if suspect material has been shipped.

- You must keep records on the condition of the test equipment.

4.11.4 Measurement System Analysis.

The standard requires that you fully understand how well you are conducting your verification measurements and the variation that is exhibited by both the equipment and the people taking the measurements. Therefore, gage repeatability and reproducibility studies must be conducted utilizing the Measurement Systems Analysis (MSA) reference manual published by AIAG. It is necessary to conduct a gage repeatability and reproducibility analysis in support of the process capability studies submitted with your Production Part Approval Process (PPAP). The authors recommend that you consider looking at the Chapter IV of the Statistical Process Control (SPC) reference manual as it will provide you with an easy-to-follow method for MSA. If you are employing methods aside from the ones described in the MSA, you will need your customer's approval.

- You will conduct an analysis of your measurement system.

4.12 Inspection and Test Status

As products go through the various testing areas as defined within your plan or as requested by the customer, the material and products must carry test identification relative to their status, unless it is obvious the location of a product should not constitute a test status. Identification can include stamps, labels, tags, records, or diskettes. Those products that fail to meet the testing or inspection criteria should be physically separated from the rest. If separation is not possible, a very clear identifier of its unsatisfactory status must be displayed. This identification should follow the product through the entire production process. These records must indicate the authorized person who allowed the proper release of the product. These records shall conform to Section 4.16, Control of Quality Records.

The standard states that:

- You must provide for a continual product test status related to conformance or nonconformance of the materials.

4.13 Control of Nonconforming Product

4.13.1 General.

Upon identification of a nonconforming (or even suspect) material or product, the item must be segregated, when possible, and identified as not suitable for use. All operations must have procedures in place to define the process that handles the nonconformance. When appropriate, the nonconformance must carry documentation that will support the evaluation and disposition of the product. A notification of the nonconformance and disposition shall be forwarded to all parties affected or involved in the nonconformance.

This clause requires that:

- You must have procedures in place to handle all nonconformances such that the material or product is stopped from being dispatched to the customer.
- Your nonconformance procedures address segregation, identification as nonconforming, and corrective methods.

4.13.2 Review and Disposition of Nonconforming Product.

The evaluation of nonconforming material must be conducted by an authorized individual as defined by your documented procedures or quality plan. If the authorized individual determines that the product is acceptable as is, or requires a regrade, a return, or is to be scrapped, the accompanying document will reject this activity and only then may you proceed to process the material. Should the authorized agent determine that rework or repair is required, the original document outlining the nonconformance must remain active until a reinspection of the material is done and only then may the issue be closed. The document prepared for the identification of the nonconforming product should include a description of the inadequacy and a full description of the activities required for correction and disposition. If you determine that the product does not fully meet the specifications (e.g., form, fit, function, performance, or appearance) but you still consider it acceptable from the costumer's perspective, a full report of the material's condition must be made available to the customer, and this condition must be recorded, the product retained, and approval received from the customer prior to shipment. Should your customer require that any repairs to the materials be reported, it too shall be reported and material held until the customer agrees to accept the material.

Nonconforming product review and disposition requires that:

- You define who the responsible authority is for defining the disposition of nonconforming materials.
- Disposition procedures should consider four possibilities with appropriately defined review procedures: use as is, rework, regrade, and scrap.
- Materials designated for rework must remain identified as nonconforming until a full reinspection of the nonconformance has been completed and the materials are found to meet specifications.

4.13.3 Control of Reworked Product.

Rework instructions must exist for the areas doing the rework. The nature and source of reworked material should be analyzed, and a prioritized reduction plan must be established. This progress against the improvement plan should be tracked and reported upon. When your customer is from the service parts channels (i.e., dealers and third-party parts providers) no rework of visible surface finishes shall occur without prior approval of the customer service parts organization.

- You will have rework instructions along with prioritized defect reduction plans.

4.13.4 Engineering Approved Product Authorization.

Once your product, service, or process has successfully undergone the Production Part Approval Process, any changes contemplated must receive prior written approval from the customer (this applies to subsuppliers as well). A record of these approvals shall be maintained for the duration of the Production Part Approval Process. This requires that all materials shipped carry the proper identification on the shipping containers.

- You will receive prior permission from the customer to make changes to a product or process that has received PPAP approval.

4.14 Corrective and Preventive Action

4.14.1 General.

You are required to take disciplined corrective and preventive actions based on any customer complaint, service failures, audits of operations, and quality records. This action must look for the root cause of the problem and put corrective procedures and practices in place that will prevent future occurrences. Your organization must put controls in place to ensure that all corrective actions are carried out, that they have been effective, and that the associated effort is commensurate with the potential risk to the customer. When an external nonconformance occurs, you shall respond in a manner requested by the customer to correct the problem.

To address this subsection:

- You must establish a documented system that addresses nonconformance within your operations. This system must not only correct the problem, but also address methods to prevent reoccurrence.
- Whereas there are usually multiple occurrences of nonconformity, a managed system must be in place whereby a severity weighting is applied with regard to resource allocations to fix the problems.
- Your corrective action and preventive action processes must reference and record the corrected procedures that resulted from this activity.
- You will establish a structured problem-solving process or when defined by the customer you will use the system they require.

4.14.2 Corrective Action.

You must maintain a documented system with records that effectively collect and resolve customer complaints as well as product failures. This requires a documented system on how you handle, track, and resolve complaints. You must demonstrate how your organization actively analyzes parts returned from your customers and how it maintains these records. This also means performing a recorded investigation related to the complaint and establishing a corrective action that will remedy the root cause of the problem. After you have initiated a fix to the cause, you must confirm the fix worked. These analyses shall be made available to the customers upon request.

Your corrective action procedure must address:

- Collection and recording of customer complaints and product nonconformance.
- An investigation of the nonconformance and a record of the investigation.
- Determining what needs to be done to correct the problem and the intended action to be taken.
- Controls to ensure the corrective action is taken.
- Follow-up to assure corrective action had its intended effect on the complaint or nonconformance.

4.14.3 Preventive Action.

You must have procedures in place to systematically review your operations to ensure compliance to your quality plan and avoid instances where it could slip into a nonconformity. This means engaging in a review of your operations with information from internal audits, quality records, service reports, and customer complaints and looking for similar scenarios inside your organization where you could get in trouble. You will need to create a plan to eliminate these potential nonconformities. Execute your corrective plan and ensure that it was effective in eliminating the problem. Ensure that the appropriate actions taken to remedy the nonconformity have been reviewed by management. This should include not only the corrective response, but also the procedures that have been upgraded in response to the nonconformity.

To meet this requirement, your preventive action process must address:

- Review of nonconformances around your business operations that affect the quality of your products and services.
- An investigation of the nonconformance and a record of the investigation.
- Determining what needs to be done to correct the problem.

- Initiation of a corrective action that addresses the root cause of the problem to prevent its reoccurrence.
- Ensuring that management reviews both the actions taken and that the referenced procedures are updated accordingly.

4.15 Handling, Storage, Packaging, Preservation, and Delivery

4.15.1 General.

All activities related to the handling, storage, packaging, and delivery of the product must have fully documented and maintained procedures.
   Therefore:

- You will have documented procedures on how you handle, store, package, preserve, and deliver materials.

4.15.2 Handling.

Your methods for handling must ensure the product remains undamaged and will not suffer from deterioration. This includes full documentation of methods and training to ensure safety of personnel and product.
   Therefore:

- You will have procedures on the handling of materials to prevent damage or deterioration.

4.15.3 Storage.

A documented inventory and storage system shall be deployed to ensure maximum efficiency as reflected in inventory turns, stock rotation, and inventory levels and a defined storage location for raw and finished materials to prevent deterioration, damage, and mixing. You must also have documented methods for the transfer of the materials. Documented procedures and methods should also include the regular assessment of the stored materials to ensure material integrity. You must also review, at regular intervals, your stock materials to monitor and prevent deterioration.

- You will put an inventory management system in place to optimize inventory usage.
- You will designate storage areas and stock rooms that will protect the material from damage, deterioration, unplanned use, or inadvertent shipment to a customer.
- You will define methods for receipt or release of materials from stock rooms.
- A review system shall be put in place, to ensure that age-sensitive materials are handled appropriately.

4.15.4 Packaging.

The operation must maintain formal and documented packaging procedures, labeling requirements, specifications, and instructions that meet customer requirements. The packaging instructions must be documented, the preservation methods outlined, and equipment used that will not damage the materials. Personnel must be trained in the packaging techniques and equipment used. The product should be marked in accordance with specifications and packaged according to customer specifications.

To achieve this:

- You will define and control packaging, packing, and markings to ensure conformance to product and customer requirements.

4.15.5 Preservation.

Preservation methods will be documented. The materials must remain segregated and maintained until the product has been accepted by the customer or per contract agreement.

To achieve this:

- You will define your preservation and segregation processes.

4.15.6 Delivery.

This part of the standard goes far beyond your basic "load it on the truck" delivery. It extends into the very system by which you schedule your product. It states that all your order scheduling shall be order driven and that you are strongly encouraged to achieve a synchronous build with a lot size of one. Delivery of the product is made in accordance with the customer contract and requirements. Special protection should be extended to support the intact arrival if specified. The delivery methods and practices must be documented and the employees trained for this task.

With regard to delivery performance, the standard requires a 100 percent on-time shipment, and you must have a system in place to track your performance to established lead-time requirements. Should you fail to meet these requirements, a corrective action plan must be put in place to address on-time delivery. This will include communications of the delivery problem to the customer.

As required by the customer, a computerized advance shipping notification (ASN) system shall be used. A back-up system shall also be established, and all ASNs shall be verified to the shipping documents and labels.

To achieve this:

- You will have documented shipping procedures in place to ensure product conformance to customer requirements after final test. Should your customers request special handling or requirements, your procedures must reflect their requests.
- Your production process will be order driven.
- You will establish a system of tracking and reporting delivery against the goal of 100 percent on-time delivery.
- You will establish an advanced shipping notification system with a back-up system.

4.16 Control of Quality Records

You must retain records that verify product compliance to requirements. Your records must also demonstrate the verified effectiveness of your operations. The following are the type of records that will need to be maintained with suggestions about where to maintain them:

Record		*Location*
4.1	Management Review	Quality Control
4.2	Quality System	Quality Control

Record		*Location*
4.3	Contract Review/Customer Complaints	Inside Sales
4.4	APQP* *: Design Review, Design Verification, Design Validation	Engineering
4.4	Production Part Approval	Quality Assurance
4.5	Engineering Change Dates	Engineering
4.6	Subcontractor Evaluation and Approved Supplier Listing	Purchasing and Quality Assurance
4.7	Customer Supplied Product	Production Control
4.8	Traceability	Incoming Quality Control and Production
4.9	Work Instructions and Procedures	Group Owner
4.9	Process and Equipment Qualification	Manufacturing Engineering
4.10	Inspection and Test	Quality Control and Production
4.11	Inspection and Test Equipment	Quality Control
4.12	Supplimental Verifications	Quality Control
4.13	Nonconforming Materials	Quality Control
4.14	Corrective Actions	Quality Control
4.15	Shipping and Delivery	Production Control
4.17	Internal Audits	Quality Control
4.18	Training	Training and Human Resources
4.19	Service Reports	Service Organization
4.20	Statistical Analysis	Production

Records should be defined, filed, and maintained to allow for easy access. They should identify the process and products involved. Record retention procedures must be documented and support customer agreements. The following are the prescribed quality record retention times.

Quality Performance (e.g., control charts and inspections)	1 Year
Internal Audits and Management Reviews	3 Years
Production Part Approvals, Purchase Orders, Tooling Records	For a period of time that the part (or family) is active for production or service plus 1 additional year.

The records must be stored for minimum deterioration, easy retrieval, and readability. If you reference records outside of your organization, you must maintain documented procedures supporting their maintenance. In the case of a superseded part, a copy of the old part qualification must be maintained in the new part file to support the qualification of the new part.

The control of quality records requires that:

- Documented procedures must exist to demonstrate how you store and dispose of your quality records, including retention times. These procedures must ensure easy access and be legible and retrievable for a specific document.
- Should your customers request access to your quality records as part of an agreement, your system must accommodate their review for a defined period.
- Superceded parts used for new products will be retained with the new part file.

Note: Quality records are documents that allow demonstration of conformance to the quality system. Retention of supplier quality records should also be part of your system.

4.17 Internal Quality Audits

You must carry out a comprehensive review of your organization to verify the effectiveness of your entire quality system's compliance with the QS-9000 standard, which will also include the working environment. This review should take the form of scheduled audits of the various areas, based on the relative importance of the operations and activities. Audits are to be conducted in accordance with your documented procedures by trained individuals (see ISO 10011 for guidance on quality systems audits). The results of the audits must be documented and presented to management personnel for timely corrective action of any nonconformances cited and tracked to ensure follow-through. Follow-up audits must be conducted to confirm the corrective action.

Audit frequency will be determined based on experience as well as the importance to the products being produced. Generally, no more than one year should elapse between audits of any one area to maintain compliance.

Audits are carried out according to a documented plan that will specify not only locations and time, but also the qualifications of the auditors, the output required, the method for conducting the audit, and who will receive the results. Audits shall be conducted by personnel who are independent of the operation being audited and who are trained in QS-9000 requirements.

For internal quality audits:

- You will have procedures for conducting internal audits.
- You will conduct full quality system and work environment audits according to a planned schedule based on the order of activity importance.
- The audits will be conducted by trained personnel independent from the area they are auditing.
- The audits will be recorded and reviewed by management as part of the management review.
- The audit results will be brought to those responsible for the audited areas. The management of these areas will take timely corrective action to remedy the nonconformance.
- A recorded follow-up audit shall be conducted to ensure the corrective action has been taken.

4.18 Training

Training must be provided and documented for all personnel whose activities affect quality. Personnel must be trained in the specific tasks assigned, qualified to perform these tasks, and supported with documentation and records of training. These records must be maintained to reflect the current task.

Your quality plan must treat training as a strategic issue and the effectiveness of your training should be periodically evaluated. The quality plan should require you to establish procedures for identifying the tasks that require training for all personnel. Training can be based on formal education, supervised training on the job, or past experience. In any case, a formal record must be maintained and approved by an authorized individual as defined in the procedures.

If a generic job description exists, procedures should require the integration of both the job description and any additional requirements. Requirements that are not included in the job description should be added to a department-specific record.

Therefore, three documents should exist: a procedure on how to develop the training requirement, the generic job description, and the specific training record that incorporates the additional requirements and references the generic job description, complete with the supervisor's and employee's signatures validating the successful training.

The standard requires that:

- You shall have and maintain training records for all employees whose workmanship affects quality.
- You will have a documented procedure for identifying training needs.
- Only trained personnel are qualified to perform tasks affecting quality.
- Training records shall identify appropriate education, training, or work experience.
- Audits of training will be conducted to determine effectiveness.

4.19 Servicing

Based on your policies and customer contracts, you will provide service to the level defined in your quality plan. All those activities performed must comply with the QS-9000 standard. You will develop plans, procedures, training, documentation, and testing methods to support the committed level of service. You will have a documented process that verifies that you have met all the customer requirements and that you have collected service failure information for communication with manufacturing, quality, and engineering areas.

Specifically:

- You will have documented procedures for all the services you perform.
- You will have a system in place to report observations of product conformity and verify the services you have provided.

Note: This element is perhaps the most understated and misunderstood of all the QS-9000 elements. If you send people out to your customer's site to provide service and repair on their equipment, you are subject to this element. To meet this requirement, you might end up having to essentially maintain an entire QS-9000-compliant system within this one group. If you are performing repair in-house, you are not subject to this element.

But most organizations have sent or will send people out to fix a product at a customer's site. Therefore, you should build in some minimum requirements within your quality plan for that probability.

4.20 Statistical Techniques

4.20.1 Identification of Need.

You are required to review your process for possible applications of statistical tools. The intended purpose is to ensure that you control and verify your process capability as well as the product characteristics.

Therefore:

- You must review the need for statistical techniques required to ensure the capability of your processes and products.

4.20.2 Procedures.

You may use statistical techniques to validate the product, material, or process. These techniques must be selected in the advanced quality plan and included in the documented quality plan and approved. Operators must be trained and demonstrate proficiency while the general appropriate population should be trained in the concepts of statistics such as variation and capability.

The QS-9000 standard is interpretive to accommodate different types of businesses. It is important to ensure that your interpretation—even some of your statistical approaches—is shared by your auditor. Consider the rephrasing of the standard in this book as a supplement to other guidance documents such as the "Fundamental Statistical Process Control" (SPC) reference manual.

Therefore:

- Where you have statistical techniques employed, they will be accompanied by documented procedures to ensure their proper use.
- Begin the selection of statistical tools in your advanced product quality planning.

SECTION TWO: SECTOR-SPECIFIC REQUIREMENTS

1. Production Part Approval Process

1.1 General.

Your organization will comply with all the requirements of the Production Part Approval Process (PPAP). Your organization is fully responsible for your suppliers' activities where they could affect the quality of your product. The PPAP is granted for the part number, the revision, and supporting processes used at the time of submission. Any contemplated changes require customer notification and possible resubmission of the PPAP should the customer deem it appropriate.

1.2 Engineering Change Validation.

It is your organization's responsibility to ensure that all changes are validated to the PPAP requirements.

(See Chapter 6 for more information on the PPAP.)

2. Continuous Improvement

2.1 General.

Your organization must embrace a philosophy of continuous improvement and ensure it is practiced throughout the entire organization and in all aspects. Your organization must demonstrate specific action plans with measurable results, and these results must be important to the customer.

2.2 Quality and Productivity Improvements.

Your organization must identify improvement activities in both the quality and productivity areas, including areas of customer dissatisfaction.

2.3 Techniques for Continuous Improvement.

Your organization will have to show competence in the following areas as appropriate: capability indices, control charts, cumulative sum charting, design of experiments, evolutionary operation of process, theory of constraints, overall equipment effectiveness, cost of quality, PPM analysis, value analysis, problem solving, benchmarking, analysis of motion ergonomics, and mistake proofing.

3. Manufacturing Capabilities

3.1 Facilities, Equipment, and Process Planning and Effectiveness.

The organization must make use of cross-functional teams to develop the capability of the operation while using the Advanced Product Quality and Planning and Control Plan. The goal of this team is to establish and maintain the most efficient value-adding, automated, and human ergonomic-friendly environment as possible.

3.2 Mistake Proofing.

When preliminary or ongoing studies indicate a possible failure, a mistake-proofing activity shall be initiated addressing the design and processes being used to reduce the failures.

3.3 *Tool Design and Fabrication.*

If you are a supplier who provides or uses the customer's tooling, you will be asked to technically assist the customer with the tool's design, fabrication, and dimensional inspection. Should the customer provide you or your supplier with a tool, then you must keep track of it and ensure the customer's ownership is clearly identified on the tool.

3.4 *Tooling Management.*

You must have a system for assuring the maintenance, storage, set-up, and full tracking of these tools. This also includes a facility and personnel dedicated to supporting this activity.

SECTION THREE: CUSTOMER-SPECIFIC REQUIREMENTS

This chapter cannot effectively address this section due to the diversity and uniqueness of each customer. It will be necessary for your organization to contact your particular customer and identify those areas that affect your products.

6
Working Through the APQP

The APQP (Advanced Product Quality Planning and Control Plan) represents a complete product planning process based on the Deming wheel (plan-do check-act). It begins with a team investigating and developing a viable product along with a plan on how to make it a reality (plan). This same team continues to design the product and the processes needed to build them (do). The team runs a pilot production and evaluates both the product and the process to ensure they meet the intended requirements along with creating further opportunities for improvement (check). In the final phase, the team initiates the ongoing production process and continues to improve the product and processes used to manufacture it (act).

While most would not consider this revolutionary, the rewards come from the enforced discipline, speed, and quality of the process. At Span Instruments, the management determined that the APQP would nicely suit the needs of the company, while not interfering with the current methods for design. The management team translated the APQP document into terminology recognizable to the organization. In addition, the management team recognized that the APQP was just a minimum set of requirements and augmented it with other benchmarked best practices. In all cases the documented process (SPAN 9000) met or exceeded the APQP requirements.

The APQP breaks down into five distinct development phases. They are:

1. Plan and define program.
2. Product design and development.
3. Process design and development.
4. Product and process validation.
5. Feedback, assessment, and corrective action.

In addition to development phases, a control plan outline is presented. The control plan describes the actions that are required at each phase of the process and ensures the products and processes remain under control. It is expected that this control plan is maintained throughout the product's life cycle and that it remains a living document.

This particular control plan is not the only method to satisfy the requirements of the APQP. Alternative formats are acceptable as long as all the APQP requirements are met. When Span's management reviewed the control plan example, it determined that it could improve upon it and developed a checklist of its own. This checklist ensured that all the APQP elements as well as the best practices upgrades were met. This checklist also served as a team planning and status tool that could easily be reported as part of a senior management review package. The checklist remained as an index for the overall control plan package, which is maintained for the full life cycle of the product and under the stewardship of the project manager.

This control plan may require the signature approval of your customer, as this requirement varies according to the customer.

The following document borrows heavily from the SPAN 9000—Advanced Business Planning and Control Process, and we would like to thank Span Instruments for allowing us to draw upon it. It represents an example of how a company might translate the APQP into a working document of its own, while fully complying with the APQP.

ADVANCED BUSINESS PLANNING AND CONTROL PROCESS

INTRODUCTION

This document provides guidelines for a quality product plan for the development of a product that satisfies customer requirements and meets QS-9000 requirements. The first three phases of the process are devoted to up-front product quality planning. The fourth phase is implementation and validation, and the last phase is feedback to determine if the customers are satisfied.

This planning process is a structured method of defining and establishing the steps necessary to ensure that the product satisfies the customer. The goal is to facilitate communication with everyone involved to make sure all the steps are completed on time. To be effective, the process must have top management's commitment to the effort. Some expected benefits are:

- Better directed resources to satisfy the customer.
- Early identification of required changes.
- Avoidance of late changes.
- A quality product provided on time at the lowest cost.

Organize the Cross-Functional Team

The first step is to assign responsibility to a cross-functional team. This team should include representatives from marketing, engineering, manufacturing, material control, purchasing, quality, suppliers, and customers as appropriate. The leader of the team can be from any department, but he or she must be a champion of the product and must be capable of understanding the issues.

Define the Scope

One of the first things the team must do is identify customer needs, expectations, and requirements. At a minimum the team must meet to:

- Select a team leader.
- Define the roles and responsibilities of each department expected to participate.
- Identify all of the primary and secondary stakeholders affected. (Stakeholders are the customer, employees, suppliers, and community and business owners and stockholders.)
- Define stakeholder requirements (use QFD if applicable, reference Appendix B of APQP).
- Select disciplines or individuals that must be immediately added to the team and those who may later be called upon to provide support. Communicate to all.

- Assess the feasibility of the proposed design, performance expectations, and manufacturing requirements.
- Estimate costs, timing, barriers, and aids that must be considered.

Simultaneous Engineering

Engage your company in simultaneous or concurrent engineering activities to speed up the design and development processes.

Control Plans

A control plan will be generated and maintained following the APQD format. It will evolve into three distinct phases:

- Prototype. A description of the metrics and performance tests that will occur during prototype build.
- Prelaunch. A description of the metrics and performance tests that will occur after prototype build and before full production.
- Production. A comprehensive documentation of product and process characteristics, process controls, tests, and measurement systems that will occur during production.

Concern Resolution

During the planning process, the team leader will encounter product design or processing concerns. These concerns should be documented with assigned responsibility and timing for completion. Disciplined problem-solving methods are recommended in difficult situations. Evaluation techniques described in Appendix B of APQP should be used as appropriate.

Product Quality Timing Plan

The team's first task, following organizational activities, should be to develop a timing plan with defined areas of responsibility as outlined in the checklist (see Figure 6.1). The type of product, complexity, and customer expectations as well as the elements that must be planned and charted should all be considered in selecting the timing. A team may

Phase I — Product Plan and Definition

Applicable	Item	Complete
☐	Preliminary Evaluation Mktg/Date:	☐
☐	Marketing Metrics Mktg/Date:	☐
☐	Voice of the Customer Mktg/Date:	☐
☐	Justification for Market Entry Mktg/Date:	☐
☐	Sales & Market Share Forecast Mktg/Date:	☐
☐	Resources Required (Invest.) Team/Date:	☐
☐	Strategic Plan Mktg/Date:	☐
☐	Benchmark Data & the Gap Mktg/Date:	☐
☐	Product and Process Definition and Assumptions Mktg/Date:	☐
☐	Reliability and Quality Expectations, Quality Goals Mktg/Date:	☐
☐	Design Goals Mktg/Date:	☐
☐	Preliminary Bill of Material Eng/Date:	☐
☐	Preliminary Process Flow Chart ME/Date:	☐
☐	Preliminary Listing of Special Product & Process Characteristics ME/Date:	☐
☐	Product Assurance Plan Mktg/Date:	☐
☐	Product Plan Mktg/Date:	☐
☐	Sign Off EC/Date:	

Phase II — Product Design and Development

Applicable	Item	Complete
☐	DFMEA Eng/Date:	☐
☐	Design Product to Achieve Design Goals Eng/Date:	☐
☐	Design Verification	☐
☐	Design Reviews Team/Date:	☐
☐	Prototype Build– Control Plan Eng/Date:	☐
☐	Engineering Drawings Eng/Date:	☐
☐	Engineering Specifications Eng/Date:	☐
☐	Drawing and Specification Changes Eng/Date:	☐
☐	New Equipment, Tooling and Facilities Requirements ME/Date:	☐
☐	Material Plan Purch/Date:	☐
☐	Quality Plan QC/Date:	☐
☐	EC Sign Off EC/Date:	

Phase III — Process Design and Development

Applicable	Item	Complete
☐	Process Flow Planning and Charting ME/Date:	☐
☐	Production Process Definition ME/Date:	☐
☐	Facilities & Manpower Definition ME/Date:	☐
☐	Characteristics Matrix Review QC/Date:	☐
☐	Process Failure Mode and Effects Analysis (PFMEA) ME/Date:	☐
☐	Pre-Launch Control Plan ME/Date:	☐
☐	Sourcing Purch/Date:	☐
☐	Pre-production Plan ME/QC/Date:	☐
☐	Process Instructions All/Date:	☐
☐	Measurement System Analysis ME/QC/Date:	☐
☐	Preliminary Process Capability Study Plan ME/Date:	☐
☐	Packaging Specifications Eng/QA/Date:	☐
☐	Financial Review Acct/Date:	☐
☐	EC Review Who/Date:	

Phase IV — Production and Process Validation

Applicable	Item	Complete
☐	Production Trial Run ME/Date:	☐
☐	Production Part Validation and Approval QA/Date:	☐
☐	Measurement Systems Evaluation QC/Date:	☐
☐	Preliminary Process Capability Study ME/Date:	☐
☐	Packaging Validation QA/Date:	☐
☐	Work Instructions All/Date:	☐
☐	Quality Control Sign-off QC/Date:	☐
☐	Financial Review Acct/Date:	☐
☐	EC Review EC/Date:	

Phase V — Feedback, Assessment and Corrective Action

Applicable	Item	Complete
☐	First Production Run Prod./Date:	☐
☐	Variation Reduction All/Date:	☐
☐	Customer Satisfaction Index Mktg/Q/Date:	☐
☐	Delivery and Service PC/Date:	☐
☐	Financial Review All/Date:	☐

FIGURE 6.1. Span QS-9000 checklist.

147

determine that not all the elements are necessary and will identify those that will warrant their attention. This checklist provides the team with a consistent format for tracking progress and setting meeting agendas.

Phase 1
Product Plan and Definition

The purpose of this phase is to determine the customer and stakeholder needs and expectations and to plan and define a product that meets or exceeds them. The objectives or outputs of this phase are to produce the design goals, the reliability and quality goals, a preliminary bill of materials, a preliminary process flowchart, a listing of special product and process characteristics, and a product plan. Inputs to this process come from market research, voice of the customer, customer input, the strategic business plan, benchmark data, and reliability studies. A final objective of this early phase is to gain management support for the plan, without which it will not proceed.

1. ***Preliminary Evaluation***
    - 1.1. Market classification
        - 1.1.1. The marketing department determines whether the proposed new product is targeted at one of our traditional core markets or a new one with which we are less familiar.
    - 1.2. Product classification
        - 1.2.1. New product
        - 1.2.2. Product improvement
        - 1.2.3. Cost reduction
    - 1.3. Capabilities review
        - 1.3.1. Is there a brand fit? Does it conform to the customers' concept?
        - 1.3.2. Price point fit?
        - 1.3.3. Design and engineering fit?
        - 1.3.4. Sales and distribution channel fit?
        - 1.3.5. Service and support fit?
2. ***Market Metrics***
    - 2.1. Market size and growth rate for each of the major geographic areas
    - 2.2. Key market segments size and growth rates by geographic area

2.3. Competitor share analysis

    2.3.1. Top brands and their competitive advantage.

    2.3.2. Analysis of products offered, depth and breadth of line.

2.4. Sales and distribution channels to be used

2.5. Expected pricing, discounts, and manufacturing cost

2.6. Expected delivery time

2.7. Agency approvals required and expected (state cost and expected benefit)

2.8. Patent protection possibilities

3. *Voice of the Customer*

3.1. Market research

    3.1.1. The voice of the customer may be heard by conducting interviews or surveys. It can be heard by studying competitor's products that have gained favor. Reports of things gone right are also useful. Mostly, it is an honest self-evaluation and some thoughtful reflection after communicating with customers.

    3.1.2. Define the customer. Who is the ultimate user and how will he use our product (i.e., what is the application)? Who buys the product and what are his purchasing criteria? Who defines or specifies the product?

    3.1.3. What are the customers' expectations for price, warranty, delivery time, service, product life, and performance characteristics?

    3.1.4. Who are the major competitors? What is the market share of each in the segment being considered? What is the claim to fame for each (i.e., what product feature or other attribute (e.g., delivery or price) makes them desirable or viable?

3.2. Warranty and quality history

    3.2.1. Warranty reports—It is important to keep warranty information in a database, which is easily accessible, so that customer concerns can be discerned.

    3.2.2. Failure Analyses and Root Cause Determination Reports—These are written by engineering and QA whenever we think it is important to do so or when a customer requests it. Such reports are maintained by QA and they can be a rich source of information.

3.3. Team experience

    3.3.1. Things Gone Right and Things Gone Wrong Reports— Such reports may be written by QA, QC, marketing, or engineering whenever an event is significant enough to merit recording.

    3.3.2. Road trips—When the team needs to learn something from first hand discussions with customers, they will do so.

4. *Justification for Market Entry*

    4.1. What do we expect our competitive advantages to be?

    4.2. Analysis of our price and feature positioning

    4.3. Analysis of manufacturing cost and gross profit margin.

    4.4. Life cycle and profitability analysis.

5. *Sales and Market Share Forecast*

    5.1. Prepare a matrix for sales in units, in dollars, and percentage market share for each of the first 3 years after market introduction.

6. *Resources Required (Investment)*

    6.1. Engineering (dollars and hours)

    6.2. Manufacturing (dollars and hours)

    6.3. Marketing (dollars and hours)

    6.4. Introduction costs

    6.5. Capital (equipment, facilities)

7. *Strategic Plan*

    7.1. The company's strategic plan, if it is developed and published, will set a framework for the product plan. It will define the target customer and the key sales points. It may also define constraints on the team that affect the direction taken.

8. *Benchmark Data and the Gap*

    8.1. Benchmarking is a systematic approach to identifying standards for comparison. It should include identification of the best-in-class based on objective performance measures and research into how this performance was achieved. It provides an input to the establishment of measurable performance targets as well as ideas for design of the product and the process.

    8.2. We must compare several performance parameters besides product performance. Other parameters are:

    8.2.1. Market share position and growth rate

    8.2.2. Financial strength and willingness to invest

8.2.3. New product development capabilities

8.2.4. Service reputation

8.2.5. Quality perception

9. *Product and Process Definition and Assumptions*

9.1. There are usually assumptions that the product has certain features or employs certain design concepts or process methods (e.g., intrinsically safe, CE mark). These should be explicitly put down and used as inputs for the design. If new technology or advanced materials are assumed, it should be stated.

10. *Reliability and Quality Expectations, Quality Goals*

10.1. Consider the frequency of repair, service, or calibration and make this an input.

10.2. Quality goals are targets based on continual improvement (e.g., scrap reduction or defect levels). Overall reliability goals should be expressed in terms of probability and confidence limits.

11. *Design Goals*

11.1. Design goals are a translation of the voice of the customer into tentative but measurable design objectives. The proper selection of design goals ensures that the voice of the customer is not lost in subsequent design activity.

12. *Preliminary Bill of Material (BOM)*

12.1. The team should attempt to make a preliminary BOM based on the product and process assumptions. This is to help identify the vendors, subcontractors, and design processes to be employed.

13. *Preliminary Process Flowchart*

13.1. The anticipated manufacturing process should be described using a flowchart developed from the preliminary BOM and assumptions from previous evaluations.

14. *Preliminary Listing of Special Product and Process Characteristics*

14.1. Special product and process characteristics are identified by the customer. The team should make sure that these are put down in a list. It should be based on:

14.1.1. Product assumptions based on the analysis of customer expectations.

14.1.2. Reliability goals

14.1.3. Special process characteristics from the anticipated manufacturing process (flowchart)

14.1.4. Similar part FMEAs (failure mode effects analysis)

15.   Product Assurance Plan
   15.1.   Outline of program requirements
   15.2.   Identification of reliability, durability requirements
   15.3.   Assessment of new technology, complexity, materials, application, environment, packaging, service, and manufacturing requirements that may put the program at risk.
   15.4.   Development of FMEA
   15.5.   Development of preliminary engineering standards requirements.
16.   Product Plan
   16.1.   Product life cycle
   16.2.   Net cash flow over the life of the product
   16.3.   Break-even time and total gross profit over the product life
   16.4.   Introduction plan
   16.5.   Training plan
   16.6.   Warranty expectations
17.   Executive Committee Sign Off

The executive committee's support and commitment are essential to the product planning team's success. The team must update the committee at the conclusion of each phase to reinforce their commitment. Updates or requests for assistance can occur more frequently if desired. The planning team must demonstrate that planning requirements have been met or concerns documented and scheduled for resolution.

Phase 2
Product Design and Development

1.   Design Failure Mode Effects Analysis
   1.1.   Design failure mode effects analysis (DFMEA) is a process wherein we look at similar products to see what has gone wrong (i.e., we attempt to learn from past mistakes and the rigorous application of engineering knowledge). The process consists of listing each significant product component in a table along with its possible failure modes, the cause of such failure, the probability of such failure, the likelihood of damage to the product in the event of such a failure, and the seriousness of such damage. Use the checklist (APQP Appendix A-1) to make sure you have covered all important considerations.

2. *Design Product to Achieve Design Goals*

    2.1.   Review available technologies. If we don't have the technology required to achieve the design goals we must look for alternatives. This could take the form of contracting out a portion of the design, hiring consultants to help us with the design, adding appropriately experienced new technical talent to the staff, or taking time to learn or acquire the needed technology in house. The important thing is that the need be recognized early and that management be informed so that the resources can be made available, or the project be re-evaluated.

    2.2.   Design for function. The first objective is to make sure the product meets the design goals for function. A number of concepts will likely be prototyped and tested. The prevailing concept shall be tested adequately to demonstrate not only feasibility, but also conformance to the preliminary specification and cost target drafted in Phase 1.

    2.3.   Design for manufacturability. The process that will be used by manufacturing must be considered in the design of the product, and knowledgeable manufacturing engineers should be asked to contribute at an early stage of the product design. A robust design will be less sensitive to dimensional tolerances and to process variations. The design should also consider how the product would be handled in the factory, particularly how it will be tested.

    2.4.   Design for agency approval. From the beginning of the design we must consider the needs of the customer and the approvals that are required for use of the product. Such approvals include UL, FM, CSA, CE, Cenelec, TÜV, and many others. There are also certain product safety standards and codes (voluntary and involuntary) that must be considered.

3. *Design Verification*

    3.1.   Verify that the product design meets the customer requirements derived from the inputs in Phase 1. This is done by the product team and is reported to the executive committee.

4. *Design Reviews*

These are regular meetings led by the design team and presented to the executive committee. It is a means to monitor progress and prevent misunderstandings.

    4.1.   Confirm the functional requirements are met in the design.

    4.2.   Confirm that the reliability goals are met in the design.

4.3.   Confirm that duty cycle goals are met in the design.

4.4.   Evaluate computer simulations and bench test results.

4.5.   Confirm that DFMEA has been done.

4.6.   Review design for manufacturability and assembly effort.

4.7.   Review design of experiments and assembly build variation results.

4.8.   Review test failures.

4.9.   Assure design verification is progressing.

4.10. Product and process validation review through tests and reports.

4.11. Confirm that agency approvals have been considered.

4.12. Evaluate economic viability and available resources.

5. *Prototype Build—Control Plan*

5.1.   Ensure that a control plan is prepared for the prototype build.

5.2.   Describe tests that will be performed and measurements that will be taken.

5.3.   Consider DFMEA in preparing the plan.

5.4.   Identify all special product characteristics and known customer concerns.

6. *Engineering Drawings*

6.1.   Sufficient to manufacture and gage the part.

6.2.   Sufficient to test and inspect the part.

6.3.   Include regulatory and safety characteristics.

6.4.   Math data consistent to communicate with manufacturing methods.

7. *Engineering Specifications*

7.1.   Write controlling specifications to help product quality planning team identify important functional, durability, and appearance requirements.

7.2.   Sample size, frequency, and acceptance criteria may be defined in the in-process test section of the engineering specification.

8. *Drawing and Specification Changes*

8.1.   If changes are required the entire team must determine that we will meet the design objectives and approve the change.

9. *New Equipment, Tooling, and Facilities Requirements*

9.1.   If these are required they must be identified by the manufacturing engineering representative and placed in the timing chart. Manufacturing engineering will document the make or buy decisions.

10. *Material Plan*

10.1.   Review for special material characteristics.

10.2.   Preliminary review to identify critical materials that will require early supplier involvement.

10.3.   Preliminary BOM review. Identify long-lead parts. Identify potential problems in fabricated parts. Encourage standardization.

11. *Quality Plan*

11.1.   Establish the quality elements required based on the product specification, BOM and general description, and special customer requirements.

11.2.   Establish the material quality plan.

    11.2.1.   Review BOM early

    11.2.2.   Identify new inspection/testing equipment requirements along with equipment.

11.3.   In-process quality plan.

    11.3.1.   Review all analytical test requirements

    11.3.2.   Confirm all special product and process characteristics are addressed

11.4.   Standards required.

    11.4.1.   Calibration standards required

11.5.   Internal qualification test plan.

    11.5.1.   Life testing requirements

    11.5.2.   Verification test requirements

12. *Executive Committee Sign-off*

12.1.   Feasibility

12.2.   Resource availability

12.3.   Margins

12.4.   Markets

12.5.   Timing

Phase 3
Process Design and Development

This phase will begin the development and eventual establishment of the manufacturing infrastructure and the quality process needed to meet product specification. The primary owners within the team are manufacturing engineering and quality control.

1. *Process Flow Planning and Charting*

1.1. Manufacturing engineering will define a schematic representing the intended production process. This flowchart will include an overview of the manufacturing process from start to finish, including:

  1.1.1. Where the product will be made and capacity capabilities.

  1.1.2. The flow of materials between locations.

  1.1.3. Logistics of fabrication, assembly, and packaging.

  1.1.4. Equipment used at each operation.

  1.1.5. Process planning effectiveness.

  1.1.5.1. The manufacturing process will be evaluated for effectiveness by considering the following factors:

  1.1.5.1.1. Overall work plan will include considerations such as minimum material handling and travel, minimum of non-value-added steps, and an effective utilization of floor space.

  1.1.5.1.2. Ergonomics and human factors will be evaluated during work position design and setup. This process will recognize human capabilities and limitations, determine a strategy for hazard prevention and control, identify potential causes for injuries and eliminate them, and monitor the process for changes that might have an ergonomic impact.

  1.1.5.1.3. Analysis of process for potential areas to utilize automation.

  1.1.5.1.4. Balancing the workload between operations and operators.

  1.1.6. Lead times for:

  1.1.6.1. Capital equipment

  1.1.6.2. Raw material

              1.1.6.3.   Other facilities

      1.1.7.   Check, test, and inspection points

      1.1.8.   Capital equipment requirements

              1.1.8.1.   Select equipment

              1.1.8.2.   Obtain quotes and prepare capital approval requests

              1.1.8.3.   Place orders for equipment after capital is approved

      1.1.9.   Benchmarking comparison to measurable performances where possible.

2. *Production process definition will cause an initial detailing of the activities required to fabricate and assemble the product. This will cause the following:*

      2.1.   Assembly of manufacturing engineering samples.

      2.2.   Assembly and fabrication descriptions, including preliminary work instructions.

      2.3.   Development of testing equipment and instructions.

      2.4.   Description of inspection processes parameters, equipment needs, and instructions.

      2.5.   Development and analysis of preliminary bills of operation and preliminary bills of materials.

3. *Facilities and manpower definition will describe and identify the following:*

      3.1.   Labor: estimated hours.

      3.2.   Training needed: on-job training and prior skill base.

      3.3.   Facilities: square footage, environment considerations.

4. *Characteristics Matrix Review*

      4.1.   A review displaying a relationship between process parameters and manufacturing stations shall be conducted. This evaluation of activities will uncover key product parameter relationships and highlight where each station that is involved can affect them. The intent is to ensure all upstream and downstream operations protect the integrity of the product parameters. Refer to Appendix B of APQP.

5. *Process Failure Mode and Effects Analysis (PFMEA)*

      5.1.   This analysis will look at potential process problems for the new or revised production process. The purpose is to anticipate product problems prior to the initiation of the production process. It should draw upon similar methods and the identification of similar problems.

6. Prelaunch Control Plan

6.1.   A description of the dimensional measurements and material and functional tests that will occur after prototype and before full production. The plan should include additional product and process controls to be implemented until the production process is validated. The purpose of the plan is to contain potential nonconformances during or prior to initial production runs. It may include more frequent inspection, statistical evaluations, or more audits.

7. Sourcing

7.1.   A preliminary demand schedule is confirmed and sourcing of materials from the suppliers is initiated along with the incoming quality control (IQC) plan.

8. Preproduction Plan

8.1.   Begins the actual physical and assembly, testing, and inspection process installation. This will include;

   8.1.1.   Assembly areas and equipment

   8.1.2.   Flow paths

   8.1.3.   Repair stations

   8.1.4.   Storage areas

   8.1.5.   Information and office areas

   8.1.6.   Inspection and testing areas

9. Process Instructions

9.1.   The appropriate departments will document and approve a complete set of procedures and work instructions. These instructions will assure all inputs such as PFMEAs and characteristics matrices have been considered.

10. Measurement System Analysis

10.1.   The team will develop a plan to accomplish the required measurement system analysis. This can be done by reviewing and insuring the gauging equipment has the accuracy, reproducibility, repeatability, and a correlation to duplicate gauging equipment.

11. Preliminary Process Capability Study Plan

11.1.   A plan and method shall be put in place to collect data and address the capability of the entire production process.

12. *Packaging Specifications*
    12.1. The team shall ensure that all individual and consolidating packages have been designed and developed. The packaging design must ensure that product performance and characteristics will remain unchanged during packaging, transit, and unpacking.
13. *Financial Review: A Full Proforma Rollout.*
14. *Executive Committee Review*
    14.1. A full project review with management. Management provides authorization for full production with assistance with any unresolved issues.

Phase 4
Production and Process Validation

In this phase, initiate a production trial run and validate the product and manufacturing process. This will cause the acceptance and full production start-up.

1. *Production Trial Run*
    1.1. This production run will incorporate the actual intended equipment, tooling, operators, and environment. Its purpose is to verify the work instructions, train operators, prove equipment, provide production standards, and resolve design and manufacturability problems.
2. *Production Part Validation and Approval*
    2.1. A production part approval will be generated by quality assurance based on an independent review by QA with equipment separate from the equipment used in the manufacture and verification of the product (where possible). This review will include a full specification and performance analysis to include a defined preliminary test period with testing and inspection devices independent of production. As appropriate, this will include a submission for approval to a defined customer in the manner required.
3. *Measurement Systems Evaluation*
    3.1. A documented review of the testing and measurement devices shall be conducted by quality control to ensure product characteristics are being met.
4. *Preliminary Process Capability Study*
    4.1. The capability study plan as defined in phase 3 shall be initiated and the data reviewed by manufacturing engineering. Inspection

and test plans shall be modified to ensure full product integrity to specification. Actions will be initiated to improve the capability of the processes employed.

5. Packaging Validation

5.1. Manufacturing engineering will initiate tests to ensure product protection during normal transport.

6. Work Instructions

6.1. Work instructions are a written, dynamic description of the systems for controlling parts and processes and are a logical extension of the prelaunch control plan. These instructions will be maintained and modified by manufacturing and manufacturing engineering.

7. Quality Control Sign-Off

7.1. Quality control will conduct a full audit to confirm work instructions and procedures, gauges and testing equipment and activities defined in the plan. This plan will meet the full specifications of the Tier I Quality Manual.

8. Financial Review

8.1. Manufacturing engineering and accounting will verify the established work standards, materials, and overheads and initiate all appropriate adjustments.

9. Executive Committee Review

9.1. A full project review with management. Management provides authorization for full production with assistance to any unresolved issues.

Phase 5
Feedback, Assessment, and Corrective Action

1. First Production Run to Satisfy Customer Demand

2. Variation Reduction

2.1. Control charts will continue to be deployed along with supporting activities that will reduce both common cause and special cause variation.

3. Customer Satisfaction Index

3.1. A survey of the customer should be initiated to assess not only level of overall satisfaction, but also to encourage new ideas with regard to the evolution of the product.

4. Delivery and Service

4.1. The production control group shall continue to monitor on-time delivery as well as service levels to repairs with the goal of achieving 100 percent on-time delivery of products and services. Quality assurance shall endeavor to review all customer returns for product improvement possibilities and respond quickly to all customer inquiries with regard to service and repairs.

5. Financial Review

5.1. Ongoing reviews should now incorporate an analysis of cost and the targets set for cost reduction.

7

_____ Quality Manual

The following Quality Manual represents a Tier I document designed to help your organization define its quality plan; in some organizations this is the quality plan.

The manual is constructed to support both the automotive industry requirements for QS-9000 as well as nonautomotive customers who may not require the same rigors or reporting. This manual has undergone extensive auditor review; however, it was designed for a unique company. We recommend that it only be used as a guide. We thank Span Instruments for allowing us to make heavy use of their Tier I document.

Quality Manual

Tier I
Revision E
10-22-96

02-001

QUALITY MANUAL
ISSUANCE DATE: 10-22-96

Table of Contents

Element	Description	Revision	Date	Page
4.19	Servicing and Repair	2	5-07-96	207
4.20	Statistical Techniques	2	5-07-96	208
5.0	QS-9000 Supplemental Sector-Specific Standards	1	5-02-96	209
6.0	Appendix A. Organization Chart	3	10-22-96	212
7.0	Procedures and Work Instruction Index	1	5-07-96	213

SECTION: 1   ISSUANCE DATE: 5-07-96
ELEMENT: **QUALITY MISSION**   AUTHORED BY:
            AND POLICY
REVISION #: 2   APPROVED BY:

Quality Mission:

The future lies with the satisfaction of our customers, employees, shareholders, suppliers, and our local community.

We will produce products and services with one thought in mind, that those products and services meet or exceed the expectations of our customers in every way.

We will provide our employees with the training required to do their jobs, a safe working environment, the opportunity for growth and recognition for their efforts.

We will treat our suppliers and community with the same respect and attitude as our customers.

Quality is the individual responsibility of each employee.

Quality Policy:

Excellence in Everything We Do Is Our Goal!

Signed:

_____

President

5-07-96

SECTION: 2   ISSUANCE DATE: 10-22-96
ELEMENT: **AUTHORIZATION**   AUTHORED BY:
REVISION #: 3   APPROVED BY:

This manual is published to identify business process requirements. This document serves as a summarization of the responsibilities and activities that allow us the ability to fully meet and successfully practice all the ISO 9000 standard requirements and meet the intents of the QS-9000 standard where practical and required by our customers. Hence this manual will be considered to support a system called ISO/QS-9000.

The fundamental concept of this document is to provide procedural information necessary for instruction and control of all operations affecting quality. It is the intention of this manual to provide guidance for each area within Instruments, to ensure it develops systems, procedures, and recordkeeping and provides evidence of successful testing and internal audits of processes, people, and products.

This document will be maintained by the following people:

Copy 1. President
      2. Vice-president of operations
      3. Vice-president of technology
      4. Senior vice-president of sales and marketing
      5. All directors, managers, and supervisors
      6. Director of quality control
      7. Corporate vice-president of quality and procurement

This entire manual will be reviewed no later than every 2 years, and sections will be updated when necessary to appropriately reflect the quality plan for our company. The director of quality control has retained a record of these updates. Changes to this manual will carry the approval of the president and corporate vice-president of quality and procurement.

This manual has been authorized by:

_____
President

_____
Corporate Vice-President of Quality and Procurement

SECTION: **3**
ELEMENT: **INTRODUCTION TO**
THE CORPORATION AND
THE QUALITY SYSTEM
REVISION #: 2

ISSUANCE DATE: 5-07-96
AUTHORED BY:

APPROVED BY:

This corporation was founded in 1967 as a manufacturer of pressure and flow measuring equipment. It has a single campus containing seven buildings located in Plano Texas, enclosing 80,000 sq. ft. and employs approximately 350 people. The campus supports the design, manufacture, and repair of products.

The company products fall primarily within four major product groupings:

- Pressure transducers
- Mechanical gauges
- Electronic measuring devices
- Contract assembly

A full reporting review of the organization is available within Section 6: Appendix A: The Organization Chart.

The quality system is communicated and managed via a tiered quality system.

Tier I.   The Quality Manual
Tier II.   Departmental quality manuals: Quality Control and Quality
                                        Assurance
                            Production
                            Engineering
                            Purchasing and Procurement
                            Sales and Marketing
                            Training
           Advanced Product Quality Planning and Control Plan
Tier III. Departmental operating procedures
Tier IV.   Departmental work instructions
Tier V.   Forms

SECTION: 4.1   ISSUANCE DATE: 10-22-96
ELEMENT: **MANAGEMENT**   AUTHORED BY:
      RESPONSIBILITY
REVISION #: 3   APPROVED BY:

4.1.1 Scope

It is the intent of this section to identify responsibility to ensure the ISO/QS-9000 standard and our quality mission and policy are met.

4.1.1.1 *The quality policy is defined in Section 1 of this manual.*

4.1.2.1 *Responsibility and Authority*

The quality program within this company has been established at the direction of the president and the corporate vice-president of quality and procurement. The responsibility for the development and integration of the quality mission and quality plan resides with the corporate vice-president of quality and procurement while the administration of the ISO/QS-9000 standard and compliance is assigned to the director of quality control and the quality control function.

The responsibility for execution of the quality program is delegated to the operational managers and supervisors. The operational managers may delegate responsibility for the quality program; however, they will maintain the ultimate responsibility.

The director of quality control oversees the quality control (QC) operations as shown in Section 6: Appendix A. The quality control organization is responsible for overseeing incoming material inspection, in-process test, final test and inspection, and statistical techniques in conjunction with the operating departments. Audits shall be conducted directly by internal audit, under the direction of the director of quality control.

Quality control has the organizational freedom and authority to initiate action to prevent the occurrence of nonconformities, record problems, initiate corrective actions, verify solutions, and if necessary, stop those processes until such time as they fully comply.

4.1.2.2 Resources

Each organization shall designate appropriately trained individuals to meet all the requirements of the quality program. Personnel performing these quality inspections shall be approved by the director of quality control.

Incoming material inspection shall verify the conformance of incoming raw material and products against the design specifications and be managed by the materials organization and overseen by quality control.

In-process inspection, final inspection, and functional testing shall ensure conformance to product design specification. This function will be managed by quality control.

Design reviews will be initiated and conducted by documented and designated personnel. This function shall be managed by the engineering organization and overseen by quality assurance.

Internal quality audits of process and products, used to verify conformance, shall be performed by independent personnel trained and appointed by the director of quality control. Personnel performing these quality audits will be able to audit any appropriate area; however, they may not audit areas in which they have responsibility for the products or service being produced.

4.1.2.3 Management Representative

The director of quality control is responsible to assure that the ISO/QS 9000 requirements are met, as well as all other customer requested requirements. The corporate vice-president of quality and procurement will provide quarterly reports on the status of the quality system and its progress. This will be accomplished via a report on measures reflective of the quality system and customer satisfaction.

The director of quality control will act as the primary communications contact with reference to outside sources affecting the integrity of the ISO/QS-9000 system.

4.1.3 Management Review

Once each calendar year, the president and corporate vice-president of quality and procurement shall review the quality system's methodology and its application to all the ISO/QS-9000 standard elements. Revisions to the manual and quality system shall be made as required to guarantee the quality of the product, customer services and the needs of the company.

The president and the senior management will provide regular reviews of quality issues (e.g., audits and customer complaints). These reviews will result in corrective action plans and will be reflected in the minutes of these meetings.

4.1.4 Business Plan

The company utilizes a business planning process based upon the utilization and consolidation of the "Advanced Business Planning and Control Process." This integration of the process includes the ongoing improvement of the products and services. The business plan shall be treated as a controlled document.

4.1.5 Analysis and Use of Company-Level Data

The company will maintain a system for the collection and reporting of company wide data, with regard to the performance of the business. These performance metrics shall include efficiencies, delivery performances, returns, measures of process integrity and employee participation. These metrics shall be analyzed for trends and review quarterly by senior management.

4.1.6 Customer Satisfaction

A set of indicators shall be maintained by corporate quality and marketing to reflect the overall level of customer satisfaction and reviewed by senior management. When possible a competitive benchmark will be developed. Indicators shall be listed within the index of the corporate business quality metrics report.

SECTION: 4.2
ELEMENT: QUALITY SYSTEM
REVISION #: 2

ISSUANCE DATE: 5-07-96
AUTHORED BY:
APPROVED BY:

4.2.1 Scope

This section provides an outline of the quality control program as a means for ensuring that the products and processes conform to the specified customer requirements and the ISO/QS-9000 standard. This quality plan is captured within this quality manual. It is the responsibility of the director of quality control to maintain this manual as an outline as well as this manual representing our overall quality plan. A full detailed listing of procedures supporting this plan, for all areas, is listed the procedures index in section 7. Each area has developed its own Tier II manual, representing a detailed response to this Tier I quality manual.

4.2.2. Quality System

The quality control program within the organization is a formally documented system of planned activities established to provide evidence of compliance to the requirements of applicable jurisdictional regulations, codes, standards, contractual specifications, drawings, ISO/QS-9000 as well as corporate quality objectives.

All of these activities are governed by procedures and written instructions supported with records of training and satisfactory compliance of products and processes.

The operational managers and supervisors shall establish measures to implement these requirements as defined in this manual. This shall include the preparation of procedures and documentation that will ensure compliance to the quality program.

4.2.3 Quality Planning

This quality manual and all the supporting departmental procedures shall be referred to as the quality plan. In addition, a Tier II supplemental document has been developed, referred to as the Advanced Product Quality Planning and Control Process. This process reflects the company's methods for the proper development and maintenance of a product. This document mirrors the APQP requirements as defined by the AIAG (Automotive Industry Action Group).

The preparation of the plan shall be the responsibility of the director of quality control and those individual operations affected by the ISO/QS-9000 standard and maintained in conjunction with senior management's review. The review shall not go more than 1 year from the prior review the Tier I quality manual.

The identification of controls and equipment needed to ensure conformance to customer requirements is the responsibility of the organizations assigned to the immediate task.

Ensuring that designs are appropriate to the requirements, the testing criteria and the ability to meet design completion dates are the responsibility of the engineering organization.

The identification of suitable verification points, development of test equipment, and clarification of those acceptability standards within the manufacturing process shall fall under the responsibility of manufacturing engineering.

The responsibility for identification, preparation, and maintenance of all records shall remain with the organization that is performing the tasks.

SECTION: **4.3**   ISSUANCE DATE: 5-07-96
ELEMENT: CONTRACT REVIEW   AUTHORED BY:
REVISION #: 2   APPROVED BY:

4.3.1 Scope

This section provides for the process by which we establish and maintain procedures for the acceptance and review of customer orders. It will also address the coordination of all follow-up activities. This process shall be the responsibility of the sales and marketing organizations to ensure documented procedures and records are in place to adequately meet the requirements of ISO/QS-9000.

4.3.2 Review

The inside sales organization will maintain a documented system with appropriately maintained records to ensure the appropriate review of the customer's orders. This review shall include ensuring the order is well understood by both parties and that the organization has the capability to meet the requirements. This documented system ensures agreement of the requirements prior to the acceptance to the order. It is the responsibility of the inside sales organization to ensure that a complete and current status with updates of the customer's order is communicated to the organization.

4.3.3 Amendments to Contracts

All organizations affected by changes to a customer contract shall establish and maintain procedures as to the processes used to amend a customer requirement and ensure compliance with the request.

4.3.4 Records

The customer orders (contracts) shall be maintained by the accounting and MIS organization for the duration of the warranty period plus one year unless otherwise requested by the customer. Documented procedures shall exist to support the retention of these records.

4.3.5 Customer Communications

All communications with regard to changes in contractual commitments (e.g., delivery, quantity, or grade) as well changes to the process
employed shall be processed through the inside sales group. All quota-
tions for products, prices, and delivery will be routed through inside
sales and a specific target set for a response within a defined number
of days.

SECTION: 4.4   ISSUANCE DATE: 5-07-96
ELEMENT: DESIGN CONTROL   AUTHORED BY:
REVISION #: 2   APPROVED BY:

4.4.1 Scope

It is the responsibility of the engineering organization to maintain documented procedures to control and verify the design of the product to ensure that the specified requirements are met. This documented system shall begin at the initial design and shall be carried through to the final product validation. This supplemental documented system shall be referred to as the Advanced Business Planning and Control Process.

4.4.2 Design and Development Planning

Engineering must plan and document each development project. Each design activity will have its responsibility, resources, and qualified relationships defined. As the development project progresses, the plan for the project will be reviewed and approved by those identified as qualified to make such a review.

4.4.3 Organizational and Technical Interfaces

The engineering organization is responsible for ensuring they receive all the appropriate specifications from our customers, the marketing team and sales organization as well as outside standards affecting the performance and quality of products. Engineering shall maintain a documented process that ensures the collection of this information and its integration into the design review process.

4.4.4 Design Input

Engineering is required to ensure a documented process that requires an investigation into all the regulatory requirements as well as any customer requirements that affect the design. Engineering ensures that any ambiguities with the design are resolved with the appropriate parties.

The design input reviews are documented and maintained by the engineering organization for the life of the product.

4.4.5 Design Review

Engineering ensures that as the design evolves there are recorded reviews of the documented design by those individuals identified as those functions or specialists affected by the design.

4.4.6 Design Output

Engineering shall ensure that the designs are documented in such a form as they can be readily verified to meet the design input requirements, that they have test acceptance criteria called out, and that they may include assembly and safe operating instructions.

The designs shall be reviewed and approved by the director of engineering prior to release. Where appropriate, engineering will endeavor to incorporate various tools (e.g., QFD, DFM, or DOE) to optimize design and efficiency.

4.4.7 Design Verification

The design will undergo verification by the appropriately authorized personnel as defined in the project plan, to ensure that it meets the criteria of the design plan. When appropriate the personnel will conduct recorded performance calculations and comparisons with prior products before the release of the design.

4.4.8 Design Validation

Upon completion and release of the design, a prototype of the product will undergo a documented review to ensure the product performs to customer/marketing and sales specifications in all the intended operating environments.

4.4.9 Design Changes

All changes to the design will undergo a formal design change review that ensures review by those identified parties in the original design plan. Should the product exist prior to a design plan requirement, or the scope of the change is restricted or limited, engineering personnel will identify the affected parties. No changes shall be made without a design change review administered via the engineering change order (ECO) system. Where the customer requires notification of changes, inside sales will ensure customer approval prior to shipment. Where automotive customers are affected, all changes must receive advanced approval, or a waiver of such approval must be received.

SECTION: 4.5   ISSUANCE DATE: 5-07-96
ELEMENT: DOCUMENT AND   AUTHORED BY:
        DATA CONTROL
REVISION #: 2   APPROVED BY:

4.5.1 Scope

It is the responsibility of each operation to establish and maintain control over all the documents, instructions, and data in their operations that are required to meet the intent of the ISO/QS-9000 standard. It is also the responsibility of each organization that calls for standards that exist outside of the operation, to maintain procedures for their collection, maintenance, and distribution. Where automotive customers are affected, all special characteristics markings shall be maintained and reflected on the automotive product drawings.

4.5.2 Documentation Approval and Issue

Each operation is responsible for the establishment and maintenance of the documents within their own domain. Documents and work instructions will be established whenever the lack thereof could adversely affect the quality of the process, product, or services provided by that operation. The individual organizations are responsible for ensuring that these documents are approved by the area supervisor and by an authorized technical individual who can evaluate the process and methods used to meet the requirements of the design or process. Finally the employees performing the task will be asked to sign and agree to use this defined method.

Each individual organization will maintain the procedures, instructions, and documents within the user organization such that each employee who is performing the task can easily retrieve the documents for reference. These instructions and documents can take many physical forms. The organization does not require a single format; however, these documents must be controlled, contain a control number, revision, issuance date, a reference to the ISO standards addressed and the appropriate signatures.

A master revision listing of the documents is maintained and issued by the quality control organization; however, the master (original) document is generated and maintained by the user organization. It is the responsibility of the user organization to ensure that only current documents are available for usage. Obsolete documents must be promptly removed from the department or adequately identified as being available for reference only.

Documents received from the customer shall be integrated into the documentation program and treated in a similar fashion as all documents. This will include prompt (within days) and timely review, release, and recording of implementation.

4.5.3 Document Changes

Prior to the issuance of any new procedures, instructions, or documents, the same approval requirements exist (i.e., signature by the supervisor, a technical representative and later the employees who will be using the document). To upgrade a procedural document, the quality control organization must be requested to provide a new revision number for update into the document matrix. When making changes, it is requested that the changes from the previous instruction be highlighted to ensure the proper changes are readily implemented.

SECTION: 4.6   ISSUANCE DATE: 5-07-96
ELEMENT: PURCHASING   AUTHORED BY:
REVISION #: 2   APPROVED BY:

4.6.1 Scope

The procurement or purchasing operation shall establish and maintain a documented process with appropriate records that ensure that purchased products meet defined specifications as well as the requirements of ISO/QS-9000. All purchases of materials used for the manufacture of ongoing production shall come from approved suppliers as reflected in the Approved Suppliers Listing (ASL). The manufacturing engineering organization shall satisfy current governmental and safety constraints on restricted and toxic materials.

4.6.2 Evaluation of the Subcontractors

The procurement or purchasing operation shall establish documented procedures by which a supplier is selected. This selection process shall be reflected in the Supplier Alliance Process (SAP). The SAP selection process incorporates at least three considerations in this order: their ability to deliver a material that meets the product specifications, the evaluation of their quality organization to ensure consistent delivery of all requirements, and a cost-competitive delivery of the material.

The procurement operation, in conjunction with quality control, shall determine and ensure the methodology employed to ensure the receipt of the appropriately conforming materials. This shall also include those materials coming from a customer-defined source.

The procurement operation, in conjunction with the incoming materials inspection organization, shall maintain records of the supplier's performance. The procurement operations shall only purchase materials from approved suppliers. It is the responsibility of the quality assurance operation to establish and maintain procedures for the generation of an ASL. Customer-defined suppliers shall be added to the ASL and controlled as part of the ASL process. These listings of approved suppliers must have the approval of quality assurance and procurement organizations. It is the requirement of all suppliers to provide 100 percent on-time delivery.

4.6.3 Purchasing Data

The purchase orders provided to our suppliers will contain appropriate information that clearly defines the product needed and the time frame. When appropriate, additional requirements such as workmanship, content, and inspection criteria will be included. As appropriate, suppliers will provide information and assistance with regard to hazardous materials.

4.6.4 Verification of Purchased Product

4.6.4.1 Supplier Verification at Subcontractors' Premises

The procurement or purchasing operation shall define how they will ensure that all materials introduced into the operations have undergone a review for conformity. The procurement or purchasing operation will look at materials by commodity grouping and with the approval of quality control will define inspection paths for each commodity. The receipt history of the supplier shall play a large role in the determination of the inspection path and can cause an exception within the commodity. Where exceptions are warranted, a separate inspection methodology will be defined. When a source inspection is indicated, it will be called out by the purchase document. With the completion of a source inspection, the material will be brought into our operations with the full understanding that it may be rejected at any time it is found to be nonconforming.

4.6.4.2 Customer Verification of Subcontracted Product

Records of the supplier's performance shall be available, should the organization's customers request them. When specified in a customer's contract, a customer shall be afforded the right to verify the product at the supplier's site. Verification by the customer does not absolve the organization from performing a full inspection to the defined methods outlined by that commodity.

SECTION: 4.7   ISSUANCE DATE: 10-22-96
ELEMENT: CONTROL OF CUSTOMER   AUTHORED BY:
         SUPPLIED PRODUCT
REVISION #: 3   APPROVED BY:

4.7.1 Scope

When a customer provides materials directly or indirectly, including packaging and tooling, for our usage or integration into another material, it shall be controlled in the same manner as all existing materials. It is the responsibility of the production control organization to control and communicate the status of customer supplied materials as follows. The production control organization shall establish procedures for such tracking and reporting of any lost or damaged material to the purchasing organization for consideration and eventual communication to the customer.

It is strongly recommended that where possible, a customer-supplied material is purchased from the customer and processed as material of the organization.

SECTION: 4.8   ISSUANCE DATE: 5-07-96
ELEMENT: **PRODUCT IDENTIFICATION**   AUTHORED BY:
      AND TRACEABILITY
REVISION #: 2   APPROVED BY:

4.8.1 Scope

The quality control and the production organization shall have responsibility for ensuring the identification of all materials as they move into
the manufacturing process. This responsibility shall ensure the creation
and maintenance of procedures and records that accurately identify and
report the status of materials. These procedures will be generated in
conjunction with the departments that handle the materials. When requested by our customers, these procedures shall incorporate traceability of components to meet the customer's requirements along with the
appropriate recording of lots.

    The production organization is responsible for the recording of im-
plemented engineering changes to the product lines.

SECTION: 4.9
ELEMENT: PROCESS CONTROL
REVISION #: 2

ISSUANCE DATE: 5-02-96
AUTHORED BY:
APPROVED BY:

4.9.1 Scope

It is the responsibility of each operational group to develop and maintain controlled processes that ensure their continued conformance to customer requirements and the ISO/QS-9000 standard. These include procedures and operating instructions for all operations and employees that affect quality. Specific procedures and work instructions are required where the lack thereof could adversely affect the quality of products and services provided to customers.

We believe a controlled process includes:

- Documented work instructions and procedures that define the manner of production, installation, and servicing.
- Use of suitable production equipment and an environment complying with governmental safety and environmental regulations.
- Compliance with referenced standards and codes and quality plans.
- Monitoring and control of suitable process and product characteristics during design and production and the designation of special characteristics.
- Approval of process and equipment as appropriate.
- The criteria for workmanship is stipulated in the clearest modes possible.
- There is suitable maintenance of equipment to ensure continued capability.

Occasionally the organization will engage in processes where workmanship conformance is not immediately verifiable. When such special processes do exist, each operation will identify these processes and initiate a continuous monitoring of the key parameters affecting the workmanship. In addition, the operators will undergo specific training and qualification for that process. Each organization will develop procedures and retain specific records for these special processes.

The use and extent of work instructions shall be offset with an extensive training program, and records can be used to reduce the detail of the work instructions where practical.

It is recommended that where possible the assembly instructions follow a box and diamond flowcharting method along with the assembly instructions; however, it is not required.

4.9.2 Process Capability

The manufacturing engineering operation shall review and document all production processes to validate the appropriate capability of the processes used to produce products. This review will represent the process control plan. This process control plan will include a review of all production process steps and testing used to validate our product designs. The review shall incorporate an analysis of the level of testing and meet guidelines established by the AIAG within the Production Part Approval Process (PPAP) for process capability studies. Follow-on inspections by quality control shall include a $c = 0$ sampling plan. When the Ppk/Cpk fails to meet or exceed a value of 1.67/1.33, a corrective plan should be in place to improve the capability.

4.9.3 Ongoing Process Performance Requirements

All processes shall be controlled, validated, and documented. Changes to the processes or materials shall require a recording of the event and a communication when a customer contract could be affected. Should a process become unstable (i.e., have a Ppk of less than 1.67 or a Cpk of less than 1.33), a corrective improvement plan will be generated. Until stability is achieved, a 100 percent inspection shall be initiated.

4.9.4 Modified Preliminary or Ongoing Capability Requirements

Where a customer may request a unique process or capability, a full review will be conducted to ascertain the organization's ability to meet such a requirement prior to a commitment to the customer. The product and work order instructions will be identified to reflect the unique requirement, and capacities will be put in place. Engineering, production control, and manufacturing engineering will administer the change and the item would be treated as a new product.

4.9.5 Verification of Job Set-Up

All job set-ups shall undergo first article verification to ensure that all production parts meet all applicable requirements. Once these jobs have undergone verification, they shall remain under statistical control.

4.9.6 Process Changes

When a customer has specifically requested it, any changes to the process or materials used to produce the product will be communicated to the customer in an agreed upon manner, through inside sales.

A product that has been qualified under the AIAG Production Part Approval Process will require a resubmission of a PPAP and acceptance prior to shipment. Changes with regard to continuous improvement shall require a prior consultation with the customer when the material is under PPAP control. A record of these changes shall be maintained by each appropriate operating unit.

4.9.7 Appearance

Where a customer requests a finish characteristic outside of the company's standard product line, the product will carry a unique identification, with the proper work instruction update and inspection aids made available prior to the order being placed into production.

SECTION: **4.10**   ISSUANCE DATE: 10-22-96
ELEMENT: **INSPECTION AND TESTING**   AUTHORED BY:
REVISION #: 3   APPROVED BY:

4.10.1 Scope

The quality, production, and manufacturing engineering group will establish and maintain documented procedures for the inspection and testing activities associated with the verification of specific requirements of the materials or product. They will also maintain the appropriate supporting quality and validation records demonstrating compliance as described in the department's procedures. All will meet the ISO/QS-9000 requirements. When requested by the customer, the organization will use accredited labs for external testing.

No incoming material will be used until it has undergone inspection. If due to an emergency, and with the expressed permission of the vice-president of operations and the director of quality control, the materials may forego the defined inspection routines; however, a positive recall process shall be invoked. This process will require a unique plan for this single event, sponsored by the affected managers. This documented plan shall require the tracking of this material to support its recall. No material may be released to the customer without the completion of all functional design and safety requirements testing.

All procedures and activities affecting inspection shall be overseen by quality control, and their signature on the proposed procedures is required. All testing criteria will be based on the output requirements generated by the engineering organization and developed by manufacturing engineering. Manufacturing engineering shall review and approve all testing procedures. Manufacturing engineering shall generate and validate all testing equipment. A list of approved inspectors shall be maintained by quality control, and an approved and validated listing of test equipment maintained by manufacturing engineering.

Inspection and testing results shall be captured within the defect management system (DMS). Data shall be collected and analyzed daily to ensure continued system compliance and improvement. Each group shall analyze this data and use it as a basis for continuous improvement of the production process. As appropriate, this data shall be displayed and reviewed with the employees responsible for the area.

4.10.2 Receiving Inspection and Testing

It is the responsibility of the purchasing organization and the incoming quality control to ensure that no materials are used until they can verify compliance with the specified materials requirements. These inspections shall be carried out according to documented inspection procedures with the appropriate records retained and in conjunction with purchasing's inspection plans for the materials. The inspection procedures shall carry quality control's approval. All test criteria will be based upon the output requirements generated by the engineering organization and testing equipment developed by manufacturing engineering. Manufacturing engineering shall review and approve all testing procedures.

4.10.3 In-Process Inspection and Testing

The production organization must generate a comprehensive inspection and test plan that ensures that all the defined testing requirements are met. This testing plan must include documented testing instructions, the retention of records that support the conformance of the product, and who is authorized to conduct such tests. No materials may bypass these inspection plans or continue to be processed without successful completion of the test requirements. In-process inspection procedures shall carry quality control's and quality assurance's technical approval. All test criteria will be based upon the output requirements generated by the engineering organization and testing equipment developed by manufacturing engineering. Manufacturing engineering shall review and approve all testing procedures.

4.10.4 Final Inspection and Testing

The production organization must generate a comprehensive inspection and test plan that ensures that all the defined testing requirements are met. This testing plan must include documented testing instructions, the retention of records that support the conformance of the product, and who is authorized to conduct such tests. No materials may bypass these inspection points or continue to be processed without successful completion of the test requirements. These final inspection procedures shall carry quality control's and quality assurance's technical approval. All test criteria will be based upon the output requirements generated by the engineering organization and include a full functional test. Manufacturing engineering shall review and approve all testing procedures. Inspections (including layout) required by a specific customer will be carried out according to a defined plan as established by manufacturing engineering. Note: Customer specified testing and inspection shall be integrated into the requests generated by engineering.

4.10.5 Inspection and Test Records

Each organization will retain records that are easily retrievable for inspection by our customers, should they desire proof of compliance. These records will be retained for three years and include the identification of the inspection authority.
Note definitions:

- Inspection. Provides for the verification of measurable physical characteristics and process events.
- Testing. The validation of a product's performance to a measurable and defined criteria.
- Inspection plan. Will incorporate inspection and, as appropriate, a test.

SECTION: 4.11   ISSUANCE DATE: 5-07-96
ELEMENT: CONTROL OF INSPECTION,   AUTHORED BY:
       MEASURING, AND TEST
       EQUIPMENT
REVISION #:2   APPROVED BY:

4.11.1 Scope

Each organization will establish and maintain documented procedures to select, control, calibrate, and maintain inspection, measuring, and test equipment used to demonstrate conformance to the specifications required. These devices include measurement tools, dies, gauges, verification software, or any other device used to ensure conformance to a requirement.

Each group shall ensure all devices, once selected, shall be routed to the calibration crib within quality control prior to their use. They shall be assigned a control number, and a file will be established for them. Each file will identify the tools, calibration method, acceptance criteria, usage locations, and maintenance schedule as well as the calibration standard traceable back to a national standard. The devices will be reissued to the appropriate department and recalled for recalibration at predetermined intervals by the calibration crib. A full calibration history of the device shall be maintained and available to our customers when requested.

When calibration devices are brought in from outside firms (i.e., rented) and they are calibrated by the outside firm, quality control shall still maintain a file on them. Quality control will maintain a copy of the outside organization's certification, traceable back to a national standard.

No employee may maintain their own inspection devices used to verify product conformance outside of the organization's calibration program.

As a general policy, where a device could be considered a possible candidate for the calibration program, it should be reviewed and identified as either falling within the calibration program or identified as calibration not being required. When identified as "No calibration required," this device may not be used to validate the materials or products to requirements.

4.11.2 Control Procedure

- The manufacturing engineering group, in conjunction with quality assurance, shall determine the measurement to be made, the accuracy required, and the appropriate device that is capable of the necessary precision. This record will be maintained in the device's calibration record file. Testing equipment will carry manufacturing engineering approval and inspection equipment will carry quality control approval.

- All the devices shall have a calibration schedule established by the quality control organization based on usage or time. The calibration schedule shall call for a date range of recall such that the organizations affected will have the opportunity to respond without disrupting operations. No department shall hold a tool beyond the calibration recall date.

- Documented inspection procedures shall exist for the calibration of equipment. This shall include maintenance and time between recalls as well as the actual testing. The procedures shall also include notification of the affected departments when a device fails to meet calibration requirements.

- All the calibration devices must carry an identification indicator noting their calibration status. Should a measurement device not be under calibration control and could possibly be used to verify the acceptance of a material, it must be clearly identified that this device is not to be used for such verification purposes.

- All records of calibration shall be maintained in the calibration file and a full history maintained. These records will include the measurement at time of receipt from production.

- Those production and quality departments notified of a calibration failure will be required to maintain a documented procedure to reverify all affected materials and if necessary the notification of the customer.

- All departments must ensure that the environment in which the test is conducted is suitable for effective testing. This will be approved by industrial engineering as part of work instruction approval.

- Management must ensure that the calibration devices as well as test software are handled properly and protected when not in use.

It is expected that if the tool is not being used in the immediate future, the tool will be returned to the calibration crib for safe storage. Maintenance of the device will occur at the time of calibration or when specifically required according to the operating instructions within the device's folder.

- No employee shall make unauthorized adjustments to calibrated devices. This instruction shall be included in the training instructions for the proper operation of the equipment or in the work instructions. In all cases, management should set aside secure areas for calibration devices when not in immediate use.

4.11.3 Test Equipment Records

A full records history shall be maintained on all test equipment. These records will include gauge conditions and readings upon receipt for verification. If a testing device is found to be out of compliance, a noncompliance notification will be sent to the user department and the Materials Review Board (MRB) will convene for a review. Should this review determine the product has been compromised and shipped, the customer will be notified and a corrective action will take place.

4.11.4 Measurement Analysis

The organization will make use of gauge repeatability and reproducibility (gauge R&R) studies using the variable range method as described within the MSA (distributed by the AIAG), with regard to critical measurement and test equipment. These studies will be conducted in conjunction with manufacturing engineering and quality control.

SECTION: **4.12**   ISSUANCE DATE: 5-07-96
ELEMENT: **INSPECTION**   AUTHORED BY:
    AND TEST STATUS
REVISION #: 2   APPROVED BY:

4.12.1 Scope

All materials and products shall carry an identification of their test status to ensure compliance with the desired conformance requirements. It is the responsibility of the production operations organization to create a documented process with procedures for ensuring that all materials and products carry a test status. The mere location of a product shall not constitute suitable inspection.

The incoming QC group shall generate a materials transfer label designating the status and intended location of materials and date of acceptance. The transfer label stays with the materials until they are consumed.

The in-process inspection stations will demonstrate compliance with a personalized approval. Material not meeting inspection criteria shall immediately be segregated into a reject area and identified as nonconforming.

The final inspection and test organization shall validate the existence of all inspection requirements as well as the test data and sign off on acceptance. Should the material fail the test or not have all the appropriate stamps, the material or product is placed in the reject area for disposition or identified with a reject tag (see 4.13, Control of Nonconforming Materials).

When requested by the customer, additional verification requirements will be established by manufacturing engineering and communicated within the work order.

SECTION: 4.13   ISSUANCE DATE: 10-22-96
ELEMENT: CONTROL OF   AUTHORED BY:
         NONCONFORMING
         PRODUCT
REVISION #: 3   APPROVED BY:

4.13.1 Scope

The appropriate organizations shall initiate and maintain procedures with the appropriate records to ensure that noncomplying (and suspect) materials or information are prevented from inadvertent use. These procedures concerning nonconforming materials or information shall ensure the proper identification, documentation, evaluation, segregation (when practical), disposition, and notification of affected parties.

4.13.2 Nonconforming Product Review and Disposition

When a material or information is found to be defective or nonconforming, procedures must be in place for appropriate disposition. The authority for disposition of nonconforming materials is the MRB, or where rework is considered, the group responsible for the generation of the defect may initiate action to bring the material into full compliance. In either case, the nonconforming material must be identified as nonconforming and remain identified until a full reinspection is completed.

The MRB will convene weekly (or sooner if need is identified) and as appropriate to the source of the material and defect. It may consist of a representative from production operations, procurement/operations, engineering, and quality control. Should a customer's input and approval be required, a representative from inside sales must also participate. The engineering representative will provide final approval for disposition.

Disposition shall entail an investigation of the defect and the outcome may fall into one of the following categories:

- a. Reject or scrap.
- b. Regrade to alternative applications.
- c. Use as is (UAI).
- d. Rework to specified requirements (this material must remain identified as defective until fully reworked and reinspected).

All decisions by the MRB will result from an investigation of the specifications. Any compromises to the materials will require the appropriate engineering change design approvals. All final dispositions will require notification of the affected parties. In the case of a regrade to the customer's requirement, the customer must be notified and approval given prior to release.

Another consideration can occur when a manager or supervisor of an area determines a product or material is not to specification and can unilaterally determine rework is necessary. A rework document will be generated and the material will remain identified as needing rework until it has been reinspected and confirmed to be within specification.

4.13.3 Rework Instructions

All groups will maintain a documented rework procedure accommodating reinspection. A prioritized reduction plan shall be established addressing rework.

4.13.4 Engineering Approved Product Authorization

When the organizations or a supplier's process has been determined to be critical and reviewed and accepted by the organization or the customer, any changes to the process or materials will require approval by the organization or the customer prior to the shipment. When under PPAP control, the customer will approve prior to shipment.

SECTION: 4.14   ISSUANCE DATE: 10-22-96
ELEMENT: CORRECTIVE AND   AUTHORED BY:
      PREVENTIVE ACTION
REVISION #: 3   APPROVED BY:

4.14.1 Scope

Each appropriate organization must establish and maintain procedures
for implementing corrective and preventive actions. These nonconformities shall be collected and analyzed, and their root causes will be corrected. The order in which they are addressed shall depend on the risks
associated with the nonconformities. Safety issues shall always receive
top and immediate allocation of resources.

In all cases where a corrective or preventive action is employed, a
record of the changes made shall be recorded and the record maintained
for a 3-year period.

4.14.2 Corrective Action

Corrective action will result from customer complaints, process nonconformances, report of a product nonconformance, and customer returns. These reports shall be collected via Defect Management Systems
(DMS) or a system deemed appropriate for the individual organization.
As a result of this reporting and analysis a Quality Corrective Action
Request (QCAR) may be initiated by any customer or employee and
submitted to the quality control organization. The quality control organization will maintain a documented process, by which the complaints
and defects are compiled and analyzed, and corrective action initiated
and tracked. This corrective action will address not only the root cause
but also the application of controls to ensure its effectiveness. These
corrective actions will be executed by those organizations identified as
the root cause source of the nonconformity. A report of the corrective
actions taken will be reviewed by the affected senior management and
the corporate vice-president of quality and procurement.

4.14.3 Preventive Action

A preventive action will result from information gathered indicating a
potential for a future nonconformity within the operating processes that

affect quality. This information may be gathered by way of internal audits, quality records, yield shortfalls, service reports, customer complaints, or any other areas indicating possible future process failures. These audits and reports shall be collected and analyzed using a system deemed appropriate for the individual organization. As a result of this reporting and analysis a Quality Corrective Action Request (QCAR (Check Preventive Action) may be initiated by any customer or employee and submitted to the quality control organization. The quality control organization will maintain a documented process by which the potential complaints and defects are compiled and analyzed, and preventive actions are initiated and tracked. This preventive action will address not only the root cause but also the application of controls to ensure its effectiveness. These preventive actions will be executed by those organizations identified as the root cause source of the nonconformity. The affected senior management and the corporate vice-president of quality and procurement will review a report of the preventive actions taken.

SECTION: 4.15   ISSUANCE DATE: 5-07-96
ELEMENT: HANDLING, STORAGE,   AUTHORED BY:
      PACKAGING, PRESERVATION,
      AND DELIVERY
REVISION #: 2   APPROVED BY:

4.15.1 Scope

All organizations involved in the handling, storage, packaging, preservation, and delivery of materials shall establish and maintain documented procedures for the handling, storage, packaging, preservation, and delivery of all products.

4.15.2 Handling

Procedures shall exist to ensure the proper and safe handling of materials by trained employees.

4.15.3 Storage

Procedures shall exist to ensure the proper and safe storage of materials by trained employees. All materials will be stored in a manner to prevent deterioration as well as support usage demands. Material storage procedures shall accommodate a first in first out (FIFO) inventory policy.

Materials that are sensitive to environmental and storage duration considerations shall have procedures that ensure their proper handling, continual monitoring, and removal if appropriate. All other materials will be monitored at regular intervals to detect deterioration.

Procedures shall be documented and maintained for the receipt, storage, and dispatch of materials to and from storage areas.

4.15.4 Packaging

The logistics organization shall package, identify, and ship the products to the appropriate engineering and customer specifications as noted on the work orders and shipping documents.

4.15.5 Preservation

A secure area shall be established to segregate a finished product and ensure its preservation. Finished goods materials are subject to the same storage and handling requirements as raw materials.

4.15.6 Delivery

The shipping department shall ensure appropriate consolidation, protection, and shipment of an order to the customer's requirements. The production control operation shall monitor and report adherence to delivery commitments. This reporting shall also include a delivery status and will be made available to inside sales for communications to the customer. The organization will provide advanced shipment notification at the time of shipment upon customer request.

It is the goal of the organization to provide 100 percent on-time delivery, and any shortfall from that goal will be cause for a corrective action. In the case of an automotive customer, notification of delivery status and corrective actions will be communicated.

SECTION: **4.16**   ISSUANCE DATE: 10-22-96
ELEMENT: **CONTROL OF QUALITY**   AUTHORED BY:
        RECORDS
REVISION #: 3   APPROVED BY:

4.16.1 Scope

All organizations must establish and maintain appropriate documented procedures on how they control quality records along with a listing of the records being maintained. These procedures must identify the record, method for collection, indexing, accessing, filing, storage, maintenance, and disposition of quality records. The purpose of these records is to demonstrate conformance to the specified requirements of the quality system and therefore must be legible and easily retrievable. The records shall be retained for a period in excess of 1 year beyond the product's warranty, unless requested by the organization's customers or where otherwise specified, such as in the case of internal audit records, which will be held for three years. These records shall include assessment records of suppliers and be available to customers upon request.

The Defect Management System (DMS), data works, and individual departmental records will be considered the primary sources for quality records and will require documented procedures for their maintenance.

A record of changes to the production process as well as Engineer Change Orders/Engineer Change Notification implementations shall be considered a quality record. The following lists quality records and the group that will maintain them:

4.1	Management Review	Quality Control
4.2	Quality System	Quality Control
4.3	Contract Review/Quotes/ Complaints	Inside Sales
4.4	Design Review, Design Verification, Design Validation	Engineering
??	Production Part Approval	Quality Assurance
4.5	Engineering Change Dates	Engineering

4.6	Subcontractor Evaluation and ASL	Purchasing and Quality Assurance
4.7	Customer Supplied Prod.	Production Control
4.8	Traceability	IQC and Production
4.9	Work Instructions and Procedures	Group Owner
4.9	Process and Equipment Qualification	Manufacturing Engineering
4.10	Inspection and Test	Quality Control and Production
4.11	Inspection and Test Equipment	Quality Control
4.12	Supplemental Verifications	Quality Control
4.13	Nonconforming Materials	Quality Control
4.14	Corrective Actions	Quality Control
4.15	Shipping Delivery	Production Control
4.16	Tooling	Manufacturing Engineering
4.17	Internal Audits	Quality Control
	Environmental Audit	MFG Engineering
4.18	Training	Training and Human Resources
4.19	Service Reports	Repair or Quality Assurance
4.20	Statistical Analysis	Production

4.16.2 Superseded Parts and Records Retention

A full history of superseded parts, drawings, and qualifications shall be maintained and referenced to a current or new part file. The full history should carry back one generation and one full year.

Quality records should be filed and maintained to allow for easy access. The following are the prescribed quality record retention times:

Quality performance (e.g., control charts and inspection)	= 1 Year
Internal audits and management reviews	= 3 Years
Production part approvals, purchase orders, and tooling records	= For a period of time that the part (or family) is active for production or service plus 1 additional year.

The records must be stored for minimum deterioration, easy retrieval, and readability. If a group reference records outside of organization, the group must maintain documented procedures supporting their maintenance. In the case of a superseded part, a copy of the old part qualification must be maintained in the new part file to support the qualification of the new part.

4.17.1 Scope

The quality control organization shall establish and maintain documented procedures for the planning and implementation of internal quality audits of our business operations and the results generated.

The audits will compare actual practices to the documented procedures and instructions maintained by each organization. All areas affecting quality shall be audited to assess the degree of compliance to, and the effectiveness of, the quality system.

The audits will be conducted according to an audit plan based upon the importance of each operation to the quality system. Individuals independent of the operation being audited will conduct the audits. It is our policy that no area shall go more than one year between audits.

Trained auditors will conduct the audit. The audits will be recorded, and all findings will generate a QCAR. A report on the audit will be provided to the management of the audited organization. The management of the organization shall initiate the QCAR process and take timely action to remedy the finding of any nonconformance. The audits will be based upon the ISO 9000 standard and where applicable, the QS-9000 requirements. This audit will also include a review for a suitable working environment.

The quality control organization shall consider the organization in nonconformance until a follow-up audit has been conducted to verify compliance. The results of the audits and recorded corrective actions taken shall be maintained for a period of 3 years.

The audit of the quality control organization shall be conducted under the direction of the corporate vice-president of quality and procurement and by an individual outside the quality control organization.

SECTION: 4.18   ISSUANCE DATE: 5-07-96
ELEMENT: TRAINING   AUTHORED BY:
REVISION #: 2   APPROVED BY:

4.18.1 Scope

All employees affecting quality will require appropriate training and supporting records. These training records shall consist of a signed job description and procedure or work instruction by the employee and supervisor.

When possible, each organization shall use the organization's documented training process for identification of training needs. The training process and training records will be maintained by human resources and training department.

No employee shall perform a task unassisted until his or her training record indicates successful completion of training to the defined task.

The training organization shall periodically monitor the effectiveness of the group's training effort.

SECTION: 4.19   ISSUANCE DATE: 5-07-96
ELEMENT: SERVICING AND REPAIR   AUTHORED BY:
REVISION #: 2   APPROVED BY:

4.19.1 Servicing

The organization at this time does not provide on-site servicing as all repairs are conducted in-house under the control of production. (Should the organization engage in such practices, it will comply with all requirements of the ISO/QS-9000 requirements. This will include treating each service request as a customer order, appropriately scheduling and tracking the work to be performed, and providing an audit of the tasks.)

4.19.2 Repairs

The inside sales and quality assurance organizations shall establish and maintain documented procedures and records as related to repairs. The procedures shall incorporate the initiation of a return materials authorization (RMA), tracking, and a reporting system to ensure all customer return requirements are being met. This data will be recorded within the Defect Management System (DMS).

The production organization shall perform the repairs and ensure that all service personnel are trained for the equipment they service.

The quality assurance organization, in conjunction with production, will collect product failure data for analysis of product performance. A corrective action plan will be generated from the returned data based upon the impact and risk to the customer. As appropriate a customer will receive a written response to their inquiries with regard to the return.

SECTION: **4.20**   ISSUANCE DATE: 5-07-96
ELEMENT: **STATISTICAL TECHNIQUES**   AUTHORED BY:
REVISION #: 2   APPROVED BY:

4.20.1 Identification of Need

Each group will review their operations for opportunities to apply statistical tools for the purpose of improving the capabilities of their processes and product performances. Production groups shall establish measures reflective of the processes employed in pursuit of our quality goal.

Each production group will provide a flowchart of their operations and identify the type of statistical tool and where it is used. Manufacturing engineering and quality control shall validate their effectiveness.

4.20.2 Procedures

Each organization shall establish and maintain documented procedures for control of the applications of statistical techniques.

Each production and quality group shall establish and maintain documented procedures and training for the control of statistical applications and the use of the Defect Management System (DMS) for data collection and corrective actions.

SECTION : 5.0   ISSUANCE DATE: 5-02-96
ELEMENT: QS-9000 SUPPLEMENTAL
SECTOR-SPECIFIC STANDARDS
RE: AUTOMOTIVE INDUSTRY,   AUTHORED BY:
   CUSTOMERS
REVISION #: 1   APPROVED BY:

5.1 Production Part Approval

5.1.1 General

Upon submission of a production part for approval to an automotive customer, the organization will engage in a Production Part Approval Process (PPAP) as described in the PPAP document distributed by the AIAG. For nonautomotive customers, a PPAP submission is not required, and a customer-specific approval will be completed as requested by the customer.

The quality assurance group will oversee the development and submission of the PPAP, along with any other customer approval submission with regard to product performance and reliability. The quality assurance organization will ensure that all required approval signatures are received on the PPAP prior to production or shipments.

5.1.2 Engineering Change Validation

All changes will undergo the full specification review according to the ISO/QS-9000 requirement, and notification will occur according to the PPAP.

5.2 Continuous Improvement

5.2.1 General

A mind-set for continuous improvement shall be established and deployed throughout the organization that will focus on improvement to all stakeholders. This will include improved quality (product and service) responsiveness of lead time, delivery, and total value to our customers, employees, shareholders, suppliers, and community.

This mind-set shall evolve from a specific action plan.

5.2.2 Quality and Productivity Improvement

A series of improvement opportunities focusing on quality and productivity shall be identified. Based upon this contribution and importance, a series of improvement projects shall be initiated.

5.2.3 Techniques for Continuous Improvement
The organization shall demonstrate knowledge in the following areas and make use as appropriate.

- Capability indices (Cp-Cpk).
- Control charts (variables, attributes).
- Cumulative sum charting (CUSUM).
- Design of experiments (DOE).
- Evolutionary operations of process (EVOP).
- Theory of constraints.
- Overall equipment effectiveness.
- Cost of quality.
- Parts per million (PPM) analysis.
- Value analysis.
- Problem solving.
- Benchmarking.
- Analysis of motion and ergonomics.
- Mistake proofing.

5.3 Manufacturing Capabilities

5.3.1 Facilities, Equipment, Process Planning, and Effectiveness
A flow layout of the process used to produce a product should be developed in conjunction with the Advanced Business Planning and Control Process which closely mirrors the Advanced Product Quality and Control Plan (APQP) published by AIAG. This should accommodate full testing, minimization of handling, and distance and optimization of space, inventory, and human factors.

5.3.2 Mistake Proofing
The organization will endeavor to use processes and design features to prevent mistakes.

5.3.3 Tooling Design Fabrication
Purchasing will take positive actions to ensure all tooling resources are adequately administered, maintained, and identified.

5.3.4 Tooling Management

Production will ensure a documented management and maintenance of tooling for in-house and any subcontracted tooling work supporting such in-house use.

SECTION: 6.0   ISSUANCE DATE: 10-22-96
ELEMENT: APPENDIX A.   AUTHORED BY:
         ORGANIZATION CHART
REVISION #: 3   APPROVED BY:

The attached documents are charts of tiered manual responsibility and personnel and department organization. Should a tiered manual responsibility be amended, a new revision of Section 6.0 will be issued. Personnel and department organization charts will only be amended as appropriate to the size and scope of the change. Please contact human resources for a current personnel and departmental organization chart.

SECTION: 7.0   ISSUANCE DATE: 5-07-96
ELEMENT: PROCEDURES AND WORK   AUTHORED BY:
         INSTRUCTION INDEX
REVISION #: 1   APPROVED BY:

A listing of procedures and work instruction that will allow a cross-reference within the organization is available upon request. Inquires for usage should be directed to the quality documentation group, where a current revision listing is maintained.

Appendix
Reference Manuals

The following are overviews of key critical manuals that you will need to ensure the proper guidance in your pursuit of QS-9000 certification. The authors suggest that the QS-9000 program manager obtain multiple copies of each of these documents from the AIAG.

ADVANCED PRODUCT QUALITY PLANNING AND CONTROL PLAN (APQP)

This is probably the single most significant document with regard to differentiating QS from ISO 9000. The intent is to cause your organization to engage in a comprehensive product planning and development process aimed at satisfying the customer. At first glance, many would argue this document is far to prescriptive and constraining, however the more you use this document, you will begin to understand that it is a "Roadmap" or "Checklist" for the way a product ought to evolve and be produced. It does not preclude a "great off the wall idea" from being "fast tracked", nor does it define a particular order in which events must occur, it simply ensures that this great idea is launched for maximum impact and advantage. The document has been built around the "Deming Wheel" of "Plan—Do—Study—Act" and provides for an excellent system of assuring a good quality product at a good cost.

The process begins with a great idea, or maybe not such a good idea, but in either case the jury will be out with regard to the merit. A cross-functional team is established to evaluate the idea and based upon its merits develop a product through to its eventual ongoing production. Once a team is established, it will define roles and expectations with the eventual establishment of a relative time phase plan. Once the time plan is established the team will move through five phases. In all phases a cost update is being presented to management. The evolutionary phases are as follows:

1. Plan and Define Program: Here your organization will establish the viability of the product from a customer/marketing perspective. You will query the customer, competitors, and historical quality information to develop product expectations. You will compare these possible products to your business plans as well as your process capabilities. Eventually you will be able to develop a preliminary bill of materials, process flows, identify special product and process characteristics and develop a product assurance plan. (Note: you are expected to use the tools noted in the APQP to achieve these objectives.) You will then roll all this data together and present it to your management for support. Should you receive their approval, the team then moves on to the next phase of designing the product.

2. Product Design and Development: As you might expect, here you go about the process of designing the product to the specifications agreed upon. They ask that you begin by looking at the prior product or a similar product and attempt to determine where the old and potentially the new design might fail. As the design begins to take shape in the engineers' minds, they need to consider the manufacturing capability and what is possible from the suppliers. As the deign develops, it will need to undergo a series of defined reviews and tests to ensure the design continues to achieve the desired specifications. In the meantime, the team will start evolving a prototype build control plan. As the design continues to evolve new equipment is identified as well as special product and process characteristics. You will then roll all this data and design together and present it to your management for support. Should you receive their approval, the team then moves on to the next phase of actual prototype building.

3. Process Design and Development: Now that you have a working design, it is time to determine how you will build the prototype product and ensure that the customer's specifications are being met. You will utilize the prototype build plan that you began in Phase 2. The team will review its existing quality effort with regard to the new manufacturing process used to build the new product. The team will build a detailed flow chart and process instructions from which the team can identify quality

characteristics that could be compromised or where a failure might occur in the process, as the product is being manufactured. The team will begin to build the prototype product from its prototype facility. It will review its measurement devices and establish a preliminary process capability plan to understand their effectiveness and opportunities for improvement when you begin the preliminary pilot production. The team will establish packaging specifications to ensure the product/materials performance and characteristics effectively remain unchanged. You will then role all this data together and present it to your management for support. Should you receive their continued approval, the team then moves on to the next phase of performing a production trial run.

4. Product and Process Validation: Here you will initiate a trial production run that will utilize the intended ongoing materials, manufacturing facility, tooling, production process, and employees. You will have to complete your measurement systems evaluations and engage in a preliminary process capability study. Your Quality Planning Team, will evaluate the product testing, packaging, and eventually sign off on the product. You will present this data to your management for approval for full production. As appropriate, you will initiate a "Production Part Approval" for eventual acceptance by the customer.

5. Feedback, Assessment, and Corrective Action: In this section you will initiate a full production of the product, improve your process to reduce variation, look at methods to improve your ongoing customer satisfaction metrics along with enhanced delivery and service.

PRODUCTION PART APPROVAL PROCESS (PPAP)

This reference manual provides you with the appropriate guidance needed for submission of your product for approval to the customer. The actual submission requires an Appearance Approval Report, Two Sample Parts, Design and Dimensions along with any pending engineering changes, Process Flow Diagrams, Tools you would use to check the parts, Material Test and Durability Reports, Process & Design FMEA, Control Plans, Process Capability (Ppk & Cpk) around key performance and safety characteristics, Gage R & R Studies, Engineering Approvals.

Another key issue to consider is the definition of a production part submitted for approval where you must first produce 300 pieces within a given time frame or otherwise seek special approval. In addition there are preliminary process and ongoing process capability study requirements that must be met. (Note: See chapter 7 for more information on the PPAP).

MEASUREMENT SYSTEMS ANALYSIS (MSA)

This document presents an overview and guidance for generally used measurement systems and the tools you may use to asses the effectiveness of your measurement system. It provides a general set of guidelines outlining two phases of a measurement system.

Phase I. You will develop an understanding of the measurement system and determine if it will meet your customer's specifications. It will provide you with information that demonstrates that the measurement system provides the needed capability as well as review of environmental factors that might affect your measurements.

Phase 2. You will analyze the existing system and confirm it maintains the appropriate statistical properties. This is sometimes referred to as a gauge R & R analysis.

STATISTICAL PROCESS CONTROL (SPC)

This is a basic primer on statistical process control. It provides working examples of statistical control and establishing process capability assessment. It also touches upon measurement systems analysis and seems to provide a better how-to than is available in the MSA.

FAILURE MODE EFFECT ANALYSIS: FMEA

This is a basic primer on Failure Mode Effects Analysis. It will provide you with a working set of instructions for an effective analysis. The authors want to emphasize that this activity should occur before the design and they believe they would have avoided many a recall or correction "campaigns" had this process been used effectively. The Analysis begins with a team systematically looking at a potential failure mode of a product; the potential effects of the failure, the severity and then they will identify the possible causes of the failure. It is compared with the likelihood of the failure occurring. The team will then analyze what is being done to control this occurrence from happening, as well as detecting the failure. A risk priority number (RPN) is assigned to the failure mode based upon a calculation (severity $\times$ occurrence $\times$ detection = RPN). The team will then embark upon a corrective action that will lower the RPN. The team will then determine if any further actions will be necessary to reduce the RPN, such as mistake proofing, training, or redesign.

Index